9 MONTHS
to crochet

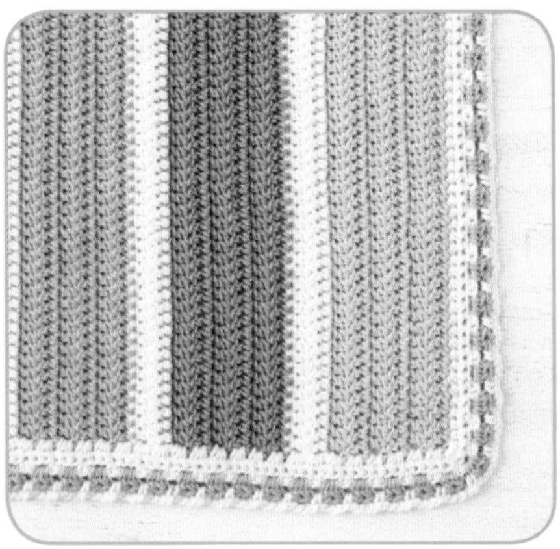

A QUARTO BOOK

This edition published in the UK in 2018 by
New Burlington
The Old Brewery
6 Blundell Street
London
United Kingdom

www.quartoknows.com

ISBN: 978-0-85762-615-8

This book was conceived, edited and designed by
Quarto Publishing plc
an imprint of The Quarto Group
6 Blundell Street
London N7 9BH
United Kingdom

Publisher: Kerry Enzor
Managing Editor: Julia Shone
Project Editors: Charlotte Frost and Emma Harverson
Designer: Blanche Williams of Harper Williams Design
Photographer: Simon Pask
Technical Consultant: Claire Crompton
Production Manager: Zarni Win

Printed in China

9 8 7 6 5 4 3 2 1

FSC www.fsc.org
MIX
Paper from responsible sources
FSC® C101537

9 MONTHS to crochet

Count down to the big day with crochet!
25 projects to make while you wait

Maaike van Koert

NEW BURLINGTON

Contents

INTRODUCTION 09

THE FIRST TRIMESTER 13

Granny square baby blanket 14

Ombré baby sleeping bag 17

Autumnal mama scarf 20

Chunky baby jacket 22

Bright nursery bunting 25

Patchwork ball rattles 29

Ribbon-tie nappy case 30

THE SECOND TRIMESTER 34

Chunky floor blanket 37

Motif nursery baskets 39

Cosy hot water bottle cover 43

Snug mama shawl 45

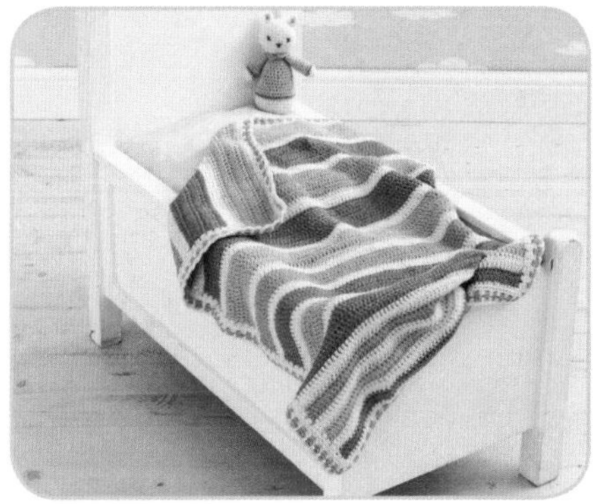

Striped baby blanket 48

Pastel waves nursery cushion 51

Sleeveless cardigan 54

Snuggly cowl and hat 58

Rattle buddy 62

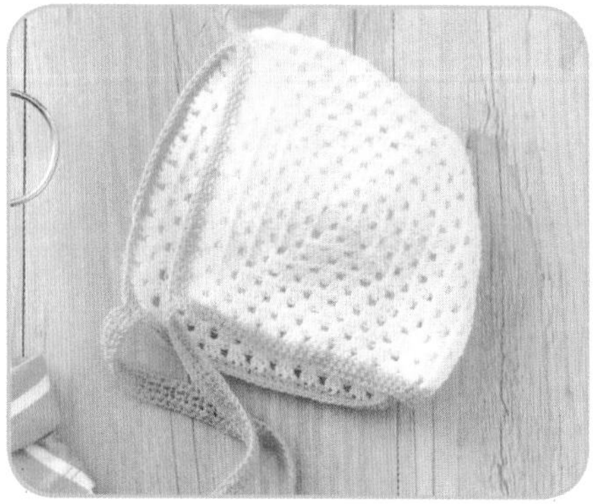

Soft baby bonnet 66

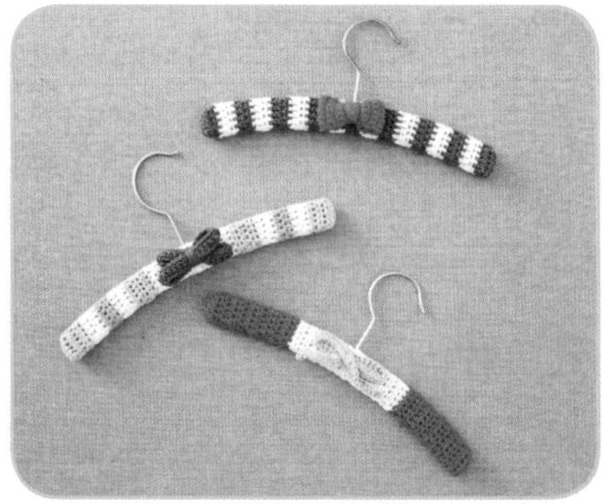

Nautical coat hangers 71

THE THIRD TRIMESTER 75

Two-tone baby booties 77

Striped baby beanie 79

Drawstring baby skirt 82

Colourful bandana bibs 85

Cute baby shorts 87

Complementary baby sweaters 89

Sleepy sheep mobile 94

CROCHET TECHNIQUES 99

INDEX 126

ACKNOWLEDGEMENTS 128

Introduction

Welcome to *Nine Months to Crochet*, the ultimate crochet book for mums to be. As a new mum myself, I thoroughly enjoy designing items for babies, the nursery and expectant mums. The utter joy of seeing your own baby wearing, playing with or surrounded by items you created yourself is amazing.

Patterns include pretty baby garments, cute toys and cosy blankets, as well as stylish matching items for new mothers, such as a beautiful shawl that doubles as a baby blanket, storage baskets, a nappy bag and lots more. My heart melts when our baby girl enters her play area and reaches out for the Rattle Buddy (see page 62). And on chilly morning walks, when she's wearing the jacket (see page 22) I made for her, I'm very proud when people ask me where I bought it.

The designs are classic with a modern twist, using colour schemes that are fresh, balanced and stylish – but also attractive to inquisitive and exploring little ones. Gender-neutral colour schemes are my favourites, and I love to play with structured crochet stitches. Of course, only the best yarns are good enough for your baby, and only baby-friendly natural fibres are used for the designs. I loved working with eco-friendly cotton for baby toys and with pure wool for warm winter projects, both practical and long-lasting yarn types. I have suggested yarn colours for each pattern, but on page 126 you will find a list of the exact yarns I used for each project.

With projects chosen to correspond to each trimester of your pregnancy, this book gently guides you through creating a beautiful set of baby, nursery and matching mama items with a personal touch. I loved incorporating versatility into a number of the designs – such as the mama shawl that can double as a baby blanket, the nursery cushion that also looks great on your favourite chair and the chunky blanket that doubles as a floor mat and throw – which will all prove useful and attractive even when your little one is growing fast.

This book is aimed at beginners but also at enthusiasts who are eager to pick up this wonderful craft again after some time away from it. The projects are grouped into three levels – beginner, intermediate and experienced – to carry you through your increasing crochet skills as your pregnancy progresses.

Chapter one, the first trimester, focuses on beginner-level projects and provides the perfect start for a newly expectant mum. It also includes a selection of larger projects that you could start in the first trimester and continue to work on throughout your pregnancy.

Chapter two, the second trimester, is packed full of practical projects that capitalize on a time when the expectant mum is usually feeling her best. There are many options for personalizing the projects, and even some technical crochet challenges for those feeling adventurous!

Chapter three, the third trimester, is home to little projects that will keep mum busy during the last months of the long wait. With a fun and more advanced crochet technique here and there, you won't be bored. And the wait will soon be over!

Whether you are pregnant yourself or excited to have a pregnant family member or friend, I hope you will enjoy working on these projects and experience that amazing feeling of the new baby being surrounded by beautifully handcrafted items from yourself or your loved ones. If you have a spare minute once the little one has arrived, please do share your creations with me through social media – I'd love to see them!

~ Maaike

Chapter One

THE FIRST TRIMESTER

In this section, you'll discover a cute bunch of mother and baby crochet projects, which provide the perfect start for expectant mums in their first trimester. Why not start small with little projects, such as a ball rattle or some colourful bunting to decorate the nursery? Then move on to some of the larger projects, such as a baby sleeping bag or the granny square blanket – perfect for keeping your newborn warm and snuggly. Offering matching mama projects as well, this chapter is the first step in building a stylish set of baby, mother and nursery items.

Granny square baby blanket

A perfect keepsake blanket, this is a great beginner's project that will introduce to you many of the key techniques and stitches used in this therapeutic craft.

Yarn:
DK weight
100% extra fine merino
(100 m/109 yd, 50 g/1¾ oz)
- 1 ball cream
- 4 balls mint green
- 1 ball gold
- 1 ball tangerine orange
- 2 balls deep pink
- 2 balls coral pink

Hook: 4 mm (US G-6)

Tension: 12 sts x 10 rows = 10 cm (4 in) square over granny square rounds

Size: Approx. 76 cm x 76 cm (30 in x 30 in)

Special stitches: Decorative stitch (see page 115)

To make the granny squares

Make 49 three round granny squares (see page 114) with cream centres (round 1) and join them as you go (see page 121). You can follow my design (see photo on page 4) or create your own.

Edging

Round 1: Using mint green, join yarn in any gap between 2 granny clusters and work 2ch, 1tr. Sides: 3tr in every gap as for granny squares. Joins between squares: 2tr in corner of first square, 2tr in corner of next square. Edging corners: 3tr, 2ch, 3tr. Close where you started with 1tr, sl st in first tr.

Rounds 2–8: Work 7 granny square rounds using mint green (rounds 2–4), deep pink, mint, coral pink, mint.

Round 9: Using mint green, start in any corner with sl st, 2ch, 1tr. *1ch, 2tr in next gap, 2ch, 2tr in next gap. Rep from * all around. Corners: 2tr, ch 4, 2tr. Close in corner where you started with 2tr, 4ch, sl st in second beg ch. Fasten off and weave in ends.

Round 10: Using deep pink, join yarn in any corner with sl st, 2ch, 2tr. *1dc around 1ch sp of round 9, 6tr around 2ch sp of round 9. Rep from * all around. Corners: 9tr. Close in corner where you started with 6tr, sl st in second beg ch. Fasten off and weave in ends.

Round 11: Using coral pink and with yarn at back, loosely sl st around post of every tr and dc of round 10. This creates a nice decorative st and defines shells with a wavy line. Fasten off and weave in ends.

Different sizes

If you want to change the size, always work round 9 of edging on a round with an uneven number of clusters of 3tr (round 8 of this blanket).

Safety first!

Toggles can be a choking hazard, so make sure you attach them securely. Alternatively, why not try using hook-and-loop tape as a baby safe fastening.

Ombré baby sleeping bag

A cosy bag to tuck your little one into. Worked in a textured waffle stitch with adjustable sides, it's stylish, comfortable and perfect for all seasons.

Yarn:
Chunky weight
100% extra fine merino
(60 m/66 yd, 50 g/1¾ oz)

- 5 balls cream
- 4 balls mint green
- 4 balls teal
- 2 balls forest green
- 3 balls charcoal

Hook: 6 mm (US J-10)

Notions: 10 toggle buttons, approx. 4 cm (1½ in) wide

Tension: 13 sts x 10 rows = 10 cm (4 in) square over waffle pattern

Size: 39.5 cm x 80 cm (15½ in x 31½ in)

Special stitches: fptr (see page 117)

To make the sleeping bag

Using cream, loosely work 57ch.

Row 1: 1tr in third ch from hook, 1tr in every ch to end (makes first 3ch post + 55 sts = 56 sts).

Row 2: 1ch, 1tr in first st, 1tr in next st, *1fptr, 2tr, rep from * to end (17 times). End with 1fptr, 2tr.

Row 3: 1ch, 1tr in first st, 1fptr, *1tr, 2fptr, rep from * to end (17 times). End with 1tr, 1fptr, 1tr.

Rep rows 2 and 3 an additional 13 times, ending with a row 3 (14½ rows of waffle squares). Fasten off. Cont with mint green, work rows 2 and 3 seven times (7 rows of waffle squares). Fasten off.

Colour blocks

Always end a colour block with a row 3 and start a new colour with a row 2.

Cont with teal, work rows 2 and 3 seven times (7 rows of waffle squares). Fasten off.

Cont with forest green, work rows 2 and 3 three times (3 rows of waffle squares). Fasten off.

Cont with charcoal, work rows 2 and 3 eleven times (11 rows of waffle squares). Fasten off.

Cont with forest green, work rows 2 and 3 three times (3 rows of waffle squares). Fasten off.

Cont with teal, work rows 2 and 3 seven times (7 rows of waffle squares). Fasten off.

Cont with mint green, work rows 2 and 3 seven times (7 rows of waffle squares). Fasten off.

Cont with cream, work rows 2 and 3 twice and work 1 extra row 2 (2½ rows of waffle squares). Fasten off.

Assembly

Weave in ends and fold bottom of bag halfway up charcoal part of crochet. All colours on back and front should now align at sides. Lay out toggles in second waffle square, 5 on each side, and attach them securely to back of sleeping bag with same colour yarns (see page 92). Poke toggles through waffle structure at front to close sleeping bag.

Close hood by folding top tog into a triangle. Using cream yarn and crochet hook, work through fptr sts on both sides: *1dc, 1ch. Rep from * to end to close hood.

Autumnal mama scarf

Every proud mama wants to match her baby, right? This scarf lets you do just that – make the blanket on page 14 to coordinate beautifully with your little one.

Yarn:
DK weight
100% extra fine merino
(100 m/109 yd, 50 g/1¾ oz)
- 2 balls mint green
- 2 balls coral pink
- 2 balls deep pink
- Scraps of gold, tangerine orange and bright pink

Hook: 4 mm (US G-6)

Tension: 12 sts x 10 rows = 10 cm (4 in) square over granny square rounds

Size: 20.5 cm x 183 cm (8 in x 72 in)

Special stitches: Decorative stitch (see page 115)

To make the granny squares

Make a strip of 32 three-round granny squares (see page 114) using scraps of yarn and join them as you go (see page 121). Try the colours used on the opposite page, or design your own colour layout.

Edging

Round 1: Using deep pink, join in yarn in any gap between 2 granny clusters and work 2ch, 1tr. Sides: 3tr in every gap as for granny squares. Joins between squares: 2tr in corner of first square, 2tr in corner of next square. Edging corners: 3tr, 2ch, 3tr. Close where you started with 1tr, sl st in first tr.

Rounds 2–5: Work 4 granny square rounds using deep pink, mint green, deep pink, mint green.

Round 6: Using mint green, start in any corner with sl st, 2ch, 1tr. *1ch, 2tr in next gap, 2ch, 2tr in next gap. Rep from * all around. Corners: 2tr, 4ch, 2tr. Close in corner where you started with 2tr, 4ch, sl st in second beg ch. Fasten off and weave in ends.

Round 7: Using coral pink, join yarn in any corner with sl st, 2ch, 2tr. *1dc around 1ch sp of round 6, 6tr around 2ch sp of round 6. Rep from * all around. Corners: 9tr. Close in corner where you started with 6tr, sl st in second beg ch. Fasten off and weave in ends.

Round 8: Using deep pink and with yarn at back, loosely sl st around post of every tr and dc of round 7. This creates a decorative st and defines shells with a wavy line. Fasten off and weave in ends.

Alter the length
Simply add more granny squares for a longer scarf. Work edging round 6 on a round with an uneven number of clusters of 3tr (round 5 of this scarf).

Chunky baby jacket

This sweet jacket is made from soft, chunky yarn, so it's quick to work up. The collar and toggles give it a smart but cosy look.

Yarn:
5 balls of cream chunky weight 100% extra fine merino (60 m/66 yd, 50 g/1¾ oz)

Hook: 6 mm (US J-10)

Notions: 5 toggle buttons, approx. 2.5 cm (1 in) wide

Tension: 12 sts x 8 rows = 10 cm (4 in) square over tr

Size: Bottom hem circumference: 49.5 cm (19½ in)
Length from bottom to neck: 26.5 cm (10½ in)
Sleeve length: 16.5 cm (6½ in)
Fits 3- to 6-month-old baby

Special stitches: dc foundation chain (see page 109)

To make the jacket

This jacket is worked from bottom up. Make a dc foundation ch of 64 sts.

Row 1: 2ch (counts as 1tr here and throughout), 1tr in every ch to end (64tr).

Rows 2–13: 2ch, 1tr in every st to end, turn (12 rows of 64tr).

Cont in 3 separate parts to make room for sleeves:

Front right: 2ch, 16tr, turn (17tr). Work 7 more rows of 2ch, 1tr in every st to end, turn. Fasten off.

Back: Join yarn in 18th st of base part, 2ch, 29tr. Work 7 more rows of 2ch, 1tr in every st to end, turn (30tr). Fasten off.

Front left: Join yarn in 48th st of base part, 2ch, 16tr. Work 7 more rows of 2ch, 1tr in every st to end, turn (17tr). Fasten off.

Joining the shoulders

Working along top edge, sew both front parts to back part, starting from armhole edge and sewing first 8 sts together. This leaves last 9 sts of front parts free for collar.

Collar

Finish off neckline by turning work inside out and working a row of dc around neckline from inside. Fasten off and weave in ends.

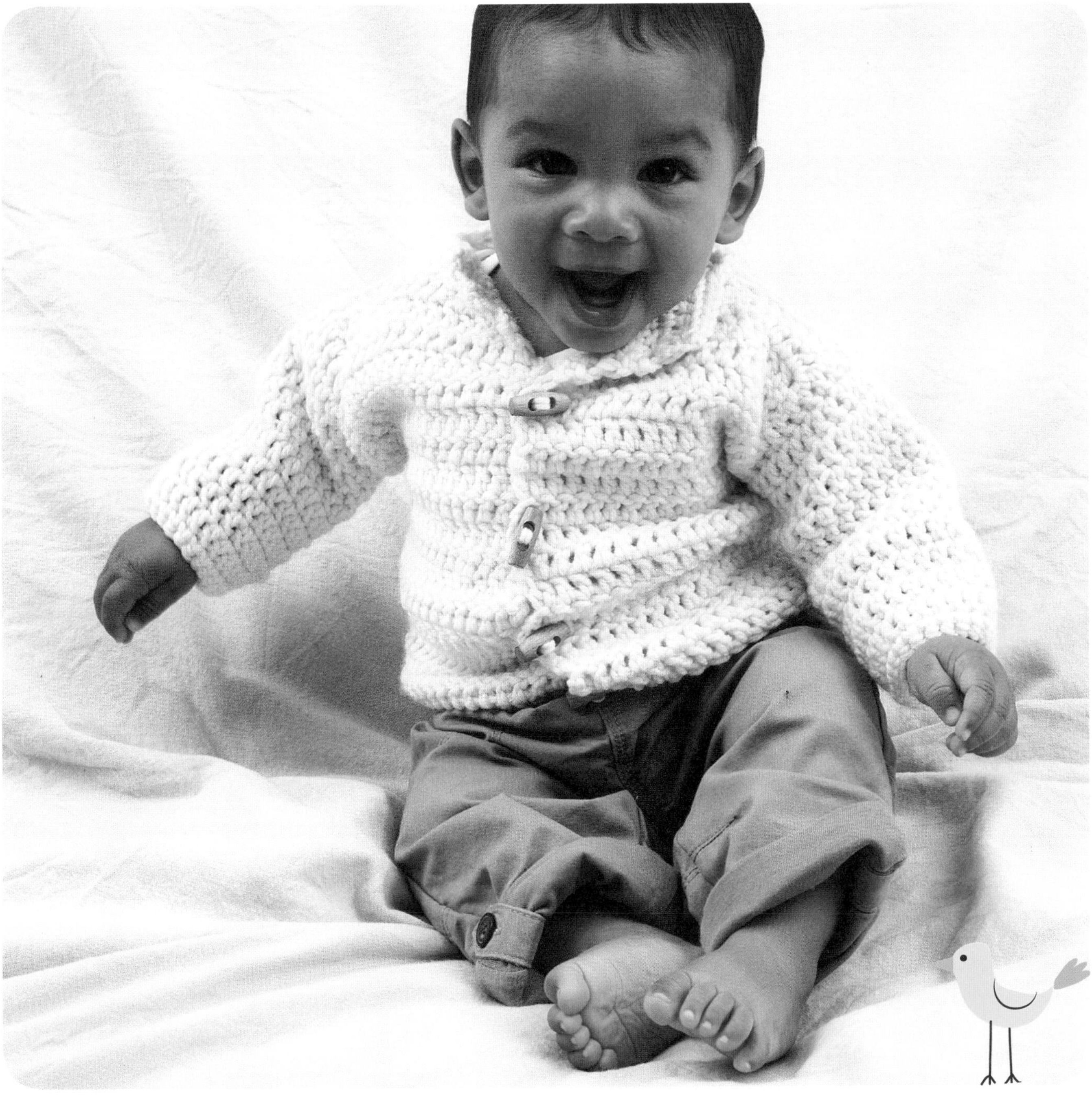

Sleeves

Sts for sleeves are picked up around armhole and sleeve is worked down towards the cuff.

Arm round 1: Join in yarn with sl st in base of armhole between front and back parts. 2ch, *2tr in each of next 2 row ends up armhole edge, 1tr in next row end**, rep from * to ** once, 2tr in each of next 2 row ends, 1tr in shoulder seam, rep from * to ** twice down other armhole edge, 2tr in each of last 2 row ends. Close with sl st in second beg ch (30 sts).

Arm rounds 2–4: Work 3 rounds of 2ch, miss 1, 1tr in every st to last 2 sts, tr2tog. Close with sl st in second beg ch (28, 26, 24 sts per round).

Arms rounds 5–12: 2ch, 23tr. Close with sl st in second beg ch.

Finishing

Finish off sleeves by turning work inside out and working a round of dc around cuff from inside. Fasten off and weave in ends.

Attach toggles securely to 1 side of front (see page 92) and close them through tr sts.

Bright nursery bunting

Why not decorate the nursery or your pushchair with a string of rainbow bunting? The textured bobbles will feel great to your baby, but make sure you fasten the bunting tightly.

Yarn:
4 ply weight
100% cotton
(125 m/137 yd, 50 g/1¾ oz)
• 1 ball each aqua blue; pale yellow; dark pink; dark blue; grey; light pink; burnt orange

Hook: 3.5 mm (US E-4)

Tension: 24 sts x 24 rows = 10 cm (4 in) square over dc

Size: Each flag is approx. 10cm (4 in) at widest point

Special stitches: Bobble of 5tr (see page 112)
Decorative stitch (see page 115)

To make the flags

Choose colour of flag and then embellish it with a contrasting yarn on front. You can use the colours suggested or design your own scheme. As you work the flag, add bobbles on rows 8, 12 and 14 following instructions for bobble pattern A or B. Alternate patt or mix them up as you choose.

Using colour of choice, 3ch, 2tr in first ch.

Row 1: Turn, 1ch, 2dc in first st, 1dc in each of next 2 sts (4 sts).

Rows 2–16: Turn, 1ch, 2dc in first st, 1dc in every st to end (5 sts in row 2, 6 sts in row 3, 7 sts in row 4, etc.).

Row 17: 2ch, 1tr in every st (19 sts). Fasten off.

Bobble pattern A (aqua blue, pale yellow, dark pink)

Row 8: This is a row of 11dc. Work 5dc, bobble of 5tr, 5dc. The bobble pops out at back of work, which is front of bunting.

Row 12: This is a row of 15dc. Work 5dc, bobble of 5tr, 9dc.

Row 14: This is a row of 17dc. Work 11dc, bobble of 5tr, 5dc.

Bobble pattern B (dark blue, grey, light pink, burnt orange)

Row 8: This is a row of 11dc. Work 5dc, bobble of 5tr, 5dc.

Row 12: This is a row of 15dc. Work 9dc, bobble of 5tr, 5dc.

Row 14: This is a row of 17dc. Work 5dc, bobble of 5tr, 11dc.

Decorative edging

Carefully weave in ends. With contrasting yarn, add a decorative row of sl sts along sides of each flag as follows: With RS of flag facing you, insert hook in first st on edge of last row at top of flag.

Pull a loop through to front. Insert hook 2 rows down and pull a loop through to front and then through loop on hook. Cont making loops in this way down to point and then back up to top of flag. Avoid pulling loops too tight; flag should lie flat. Fasten off and weave in ends.

Assembly

Make string for bunting with pale yellow yarn by crocheting a string of ch50. Then, starting with dark blue triangle (or chosen colour), attach each flag, with RS facing you, by working dc sts around tr posts of last row. Work directly into next flag without any sts in between. When all flags are attached, crochet another string of 50 ch sts. Fasten off and weave in ends.

7

Patchwork ball rattles

A simple rattle with a fun motif. Enjoy picking colours that match your style and other crocheted projects.

Yarn:
4 ply weight
100% cotton
(125 m/137 yd, 50 g/1¾ oz)
For blue-green ball: 1 ball each light blue; pale yellow; white; pale green; dark blue; aqua blue
For multicoloured ball: 1 ball each light pink; pale green; dark pink; light blue; pale yellow; white

Hook: 3.5 mm (US E-4)

Notions: Polyester toy stuffing, safety rattle

Tension: Motif measures 7 cm (2¾ in) across centre from point to straight edge

Size: 37 cm (14½ in) circumference when stuffed

To make the motifs

Make 2 motifs in each colour per ball.

Using colour of choice, 4ch. Close into a circle with sl st.

Round 1: 3ch (counts as 1tr and 1ch), working into circle: *2tr, 1ch, rep from * 3 times, 1tr, close with sl st in second beg ch.

Round 2: In first 1ch sp: 1dc, 2ch, 1tr. 1tr in each of next 2tr. *In next 1ch sp: 1tr, 1ch, 1tr. 1tr in each of next 2tr. Rep from * 3 times. Close with sl st in first beg ch.

Round 3: In first 1ch sp: 1dc, 2ch, 1tr. 1tr in each of next 4tr. *In next 1ch sp, 1tr 1, 1ch, 1tr. 1tr in each of next 4tr. Rep from * 3 times. Close with sl st in first beg ch. Fasten off and weave in ends.

Assembly

Divide 12 motifs into 2 groups of 6. Arrange each group of 6 as follows: place 1 motif in centre with 5 motifs around it, matching sides of each motif to its neighbours. Using white yarn, sew motifs together with RS facing out and stitching through back loop only of crochet sts. Place 2 halves of ball tog and sew tog, leaving 2 sides of last motif open. Add stuffing and rattle, burying rattle in centre, and sew gap closed. Weave in ends.

Ribbon-tie nappy case

This nappy case, designed to look just like a stylish clutch, can be made to match your wardrobe. Worked with special decorative stitches, it is great fun to make, too.

Yarn:
DK weight
100% cotton
(84 m/92 yd, 50 g/1¾ oz)
- 1 ball each white; light blue; beige; lime green
- 3 balls navy

Hook: 4 mm (US G-6)

Notions: 59.5 cm (23½ in) length of 2.5 cm (1 in) wide satin ribbon

Tension: 17 sts x 13 rows = 10 cm (4 in) square over htr

Size: 25.5 cm x 18 cm (10 in x 7 in) when closed

Special stitches: Spike stitch (see page 116)
Back loop (see page 118)

To make the granny squares

Start in middle of cover with a strip of 5 two round granny squares (see page 114), joining them as you go (see page 121). Start in centre with a white square and join light blue squares to both left and right sides of it. Add beige squares to both light blue sides.

First side

Row 1: Using navy, start in top right corner of a beige square and crochet along long side of granny square strip: 2ch, 2htr in corner, *1htr in back loop of each of next 6 sts, 1htr in each of next 2 granny square corners, rep from * 3 times. 1htr in back loop of each of next 6 sts, 2htr in last corner (42 sts).

Rows 2–7: Turn, 2ch (does not count as a st here and throughout), 42htr (6 rows).

Row 8: To create gap for ribbon tie, turn, 2ch, 18htr, 6ch, miss 6 sts, 18htr.

Row 9: Turn, 2ch, 18htr, 6htr in 6ch sp, 18htr.

Rows 10 and 11: Turn, 2ch, 42htr (2 rows).

Rows 12 and 13: Rep rows 8 and 9.

Row 14: Turn, 1ch, 2dc. *3ch, miss 3, 3htr, rep from * once. 3ch, miss 3, 8dc. **3ch, miss 3, 3htr, rep from ** once. 3ch, miss 3, 2dc. Fasten off.

Row 15: Using light blue, 1ch, 2dc, work spike sts of 3htr in htr 2 rows below. *3ch, miss 3, 3htr in htr 2 rows below, rep from * once, 8dc. **3htr in htr 2 rows below, 3ch, miss 3, rep from ** once. 3htr, 2dc.

Row 16: Turn, 1ch, 2dc. *3ch, miss 3, 3htr in htr 2 rows below, rep from * once. 3ch, miss 3, 8dc. **3ch, miss 3, 3htr 2 rows below, rep from ** once. 3ch, miss 3, 2dc. Fasten off.

Rows 17 and 18: Using white, rep rows 15 and 16. Fasten off.

Row 19: Using navy, turn, 1ch, 2dc, 3htr in htr 2 rows below. *3dc, 3htr in htr 2 rows below, rep from * once, 8dc. **3htr in htr 2 rows below, 3dc, rep from ** once, 3htr, 2dc.

Rows 20–25: Turn, 2ch, 42htr (6 rows). Fasten off.

Rows 26–31: Using beige, turn, 2ch, 42htr (6 rows). Fasten off.

Rows 32–37: Using lime green, turn, 2ch, 42htr (6 rows). Fasten off.

Rows 38 and 39: Using white, turn, 2ch, 42htr (2 rows). Fasten off. This side of cover is complete.

Second side

Make other side of cover along opposite side of granny squares, following patt for first side but omitting decorative spike st as follows:

Rows 1–13: Using navy, rep rows 1–13 of first side patt.

Rows 14 and 15: Turn, 2ch, 42htr (2 rows). Fasten off.

Rows 16–25: Using beige, turn, 2ch, 42htr (10 rows). Fasten off.

Rows 26–29: Using white, turn, 2ch, 42htr (4 rows). Fasten off.

Rows 30–35: Using lime green, turn, 2ch, 42htr (6 rows). Fasten off.

Rows 36–38: Using light blue, turn, 2ch, 42htr (3 rows). Fasten off.

Row 39: Using navy, turn, 2ch, 42htr (1 row). DON'T fasten off, but cont with 3ch, 1dc in corner st on side. Cont along this side with 2dc in every row end, 1dc in every st of square in middle. In corner: 1dc, 3ch. 1htr in every st along top. Cont like this all around. End with 2dc in last row end, 3ch, sl st in first htr. Fasten off and weave in ends.

Assembly

Lay piece flat, with RS facing you. Fold both ends in until they meet edges of granny squares in middle; squares should still be visible. Now close cover with navy yarn by working sl st in both outside loops of sts along sides. Close all 4 sides individually. Fasten off, weave in ends and turn cover RS out. Thread ribbon through loops and tie into a bow.

Chapter Two

THE SECOND TRIMESTER

At this stage of your pregnancy, you can capitalize on your higher energy levels to get ready for your forthcoming arrival. With a range of practical projects, including a chunky floor blanket, nursery cushion, comforting hot water bottle cover and clever storage baskets, you can start to build a unique collection of personalized accessories. Why not adapt the colour schemes in the projects to match your home decor and personal style?

Chunky floor blanket

A large and comfy blanket for keeping baby warm on cold winter days. Folded double, this would make a nice play rug.

Yarn:
Super chunky
70% wool/30% alpaca
(80 m/87 yd, 100 g/3½ oz)
- 2 balls pale pink
- 6 balls grey
- 2 balls charcoal
- 5 balls ecru

Hook: 10 mm (US N-15)

Tension: 7 sts x 4½ rows = 10 cm (4 in) square over tr

Size: 119.5 cm x 119.5 cm (47 in x 47 in)

Special stitches: fptr (see page 117)

To make the blocks

Make 3 blocks of each colour combination, 9 in total: pale pink/grey, grey/charcoal, charcoal/pale pink. Using first colour, work 21ch. Starting in third ch from hook, 19tr.

Rows 1–5: Turn, 2ch (does not count as st here and throughout), 20tr. After row 5, fasten off and weave in ends.

Rows 6–10: Using second colour, turn, 2ch, 20tr. After row 10, fasten off and weave in ends.

Block edging

Round 11: Using ecru, join in yarn in any tr along row 10. 2ch, 1tr in every st. Corners: 3ch, 2tr in every row end. This makes a square of 20 x 20tr with 3ch in corners. Close with sl st in first tr.

Round 12: 2ch, 1tr in every st. Corners: in ch-3 loop of row 11, work 2tr, 3ch, 2tr. This makes a square of 24 x 24tr with 3ch in corners. Close with sl st in first tr. Fasten off and weave in ends.

Joining

Join blocks using grey yarn. Lay out blocks, referring to photo opposite or according to preference. Hold blocks with RS facing out. Starting in middle chain of 3ch in corner, picking up inside loops of sts of both blocks, dc to next corner and cont straight with next 2 blocks. Join first 6 blocks in this way. To join final 3 blocks, work in same direction and dc as first row of blocks. Then close other sides in same way. Fasten off and weave in ends.

Edging

Round 1: Using grey, join yarn with sl st in back loop of fifth tr before any corner. 2ch, 1htr in back loop of every st. Corners: 1htr in first ch, 3htr in second ch, 1htr in last ch. Cont around and close with sl st in first htr.

Round 2: 2ch, 1htr, *1fptr and miss that st, 2htr, rep from * all around. End rep with 1htr before corner and beg with 2htr after corner. In 3htr at corner: (1htr and 1fptr in same st) 3 times. Close with sl st in first htr.

Round 3: 2ch, *1fptr around fptr below and miss that st, 2htr, rep from * all around. End rep with 2htr before corner and beg with 1fptr after corner. In corners: (1fptr around fptr below and miss that st, 2htr in next st) twice. Close with sl st in first fptr.

Round 4: 2ch, *1fptr around fptr below and miss that st, 2htr, rep from * all around. End rep with 2htr before corner and beg with 1fptr after corner. In corners: (1fptr around fptr below and miss that st, 2htr in next st, 1htr in next st) twice. Close with sl st in first fptr. Fasten off and weave in ends. Block blanket lightly (see page 122).

Motif nursery baskets

Storage baskets come in handy everywhere, but especially in the nursery. Get creative with the embroidery stitches; little motifs or baby's initials are always nice.

Yarn:
Super chunky
70% wool/30% alpaca
(80 m/87 yd, 100 g/3½ oz)

- 1 ball charcoal
- 1 ball pale pink
- Scraps of ecru and grey

Hook: 8 mm (US L-11)

Notions: Stitch marker

Tension: 10 sts x 12 rows = 10 cm (4 in) square over dc

Size: Charcoal basket:
18.5 cm (7¼ in) circumference, 10 cm (4 in) height
Pink basket: 14.5 cm (5¾ in) circumference, 11.5 cm (4½ in) height

To make the charcoal basket

Using charcoal, work 3ch and close into a circle with sl st.

Round 1: 1ch, 6dc in circle. Close with sl st in first dc (6 sts). You may want to keep track of rounds at this point by marking first st with a st marker.

Round 2: 1ch, 2dc in every st. Close with sl st in first dc (12 sts).

Round 3: 1ch, *1dc, 2dc in next st, rep from * all around. Close with sl st in first dc (18 sts).

Round 4: 1ch, *2dc, 2dc in next st, rep from * all around. Close with sl st in first dc (24 sts).

Round 5: 1ch, *3dc, 2dc in next st, rep from * all around. Close with sl st in first dc (30 sts).

Round 6: 1ch, *4dc, 2dc in next st, rep from * all around. Close with sl st in first dc (36 sts).

Round 7: 1ch, *5dc, 2dc in next st, rep from * all around. Close with sl st in first dc (42 sts).

Round 8: 1ch, *6dc, 2dc in next st, rep from * all around. Close with sl st in first dc (48 sts).

Round 9: 1ch, *7dc, 2dc in next st, rep from * all around. Close with sl st in first dc (54 sts).

Rounds 10–17: 8 rounds of 54dc. Work in continuous rounds in spiral style by not closing with a sl st at end of each round.

Charcoal basket hook: 6ch, 1dc in last st, turn, 9dc around 6ch sp. Fasten off and weave in ends.

Embroidery

Using grey yarn, cross-stitch (see page 122) a zigzag motif all around basket, starting in third row from top, working down 4 sts, and back up.

To make the pink basket

Using pale pink, start as for charcoal basket until round 7 (42 sts). You may want to keep track of rounds by marking first st with a st marker.

Rounds 8–17: 10 rounds of 42dc. Work in continuous rounds in spiral style by not closing with a sl st at end of each round.

Pink basket hook: 6ch, 1dc in last st, turn, 9dc around 6ch sp. Fasten off and weave in ends.

Embroidery

Using ecru yarn, cross-stitch a heart shape, starting in third row from top.

Cosy hot water bottle cover

Hot water bottles are ideal for soothing away pregnancy aches and pains and this soft, woolly cover will make yours even more comforting.

Yarn:
Super chunky
70% wool/30% alpaca
(80 m/87 yd, 100 g/3½ oz)
- 2 balls charcoal
- 2 balls pale pink
- 5 balls ecru
- 6 balls grey

Hook: 10 mm (US N-15)

Tension: 7 sts x 4½ rows = 10 cm (4 in) square over tr

Size: 21.5 cm x 29 cm
(8½ in x 11½ in)
Fits regular size hot water bottle

Special stitches: fptr (see page 117)
Back loop (see page 118)

To make the cover

Using charcoal, work 13ch.

Row 1: Starting in third ch from hook, 11htr.

Rows 2–7: Turn, 2ch (does not count as a st here and throughout), 12htr. Fasten off and weave in ends.

Rows 8–14: Turn, using pale pink, 2ch, 12htr. Fasten off and weave in ends.

Edging for panel piece

Using ecru, join yarn with sl st in any st along charcoal bottom. 2ch, 1htr in every st. 3htr around corner, alternate 1 and 2htr in every row end. Close with sl st in first htr. Add another round of htr, starting with 2ch and making 3htr in middle corner st of first round. Close with sl st in first htr. Fasten off and weave in ends.

Make another piece like this, starting with pale pink and then charcoal.

Assembly and neck

Using grey, join panels by working dc from fourth st before top corner, picking up only inside loops of sts, going around sides and base up to next top corner, and cont for 4 sts after that corner. Do not fasten off.

Round 1: 2ch, 1htr in back loop of 9 sts across other side, 1htr in join, 1htr in 9 sts at back, 1htr in join. Close with sl st in first htr.

Rounds 2–4: 2ch, *2htr, 1fptr, rep from * 6 times. Close with sl st in first htr. Fasten off and weave in ends.

And relax...

Fold the bottle into the cover when empty, then fill with water and enjoy!

Snug mama shawl

Keep warm and cosy during your pregnancy with this snug triangular shawl to wrap around your shoulders.

Yarn:
Aran weight
55% wool/33% acrylic/
12% cashmere
(90 m/98 yd, 50 g/1¾ oz)

- 6 balls aqua blue
- 2 balls dark blue
- 1 ball peach

Hook: 6 mm (US J-10)

Tension: 12 sts x 11 rows = 10 cm (4 in) square over htr

Size: 99 cm x 145 cm (39 in x 57 in) at widest point

Special stitches: Bobble of 4htr (see page 111)

To make the shawl

Using aqua blue, work 3ch and close into a circle with sl st.

Row 1: 2ch, 3htr in circle.

Row 2: Turn, 2ch (does not count as a st here and throughout), 2htr in first st, 1htr, 2htr in last st (5 sts).

Rows 3–71: Turn, 2ch, 2htr in first st, 1htr in every st to last st, 2htr in last st (7 sts in row 3, 9 sts in row 4, 11 sts in row 5, etc.) – (143 sts).

Edging

After row 71, don't fasten off but cont along sides of triangle with 3ch, 2htr in every row end. At bottom point: 2htr, 2ch, 2htr. When you reach other top corner, 3ch and close with sl st in first htr of that top row. Fasten off and weave in ends.

Using dark blue, join yarn with sl st in any st along top of shawl. 2ch, 1htr in back loop of every st. All 3 corners: 4htr in 3ch sp of previous row. Close with sl st in first htr. Fasten off and weave in ends.

Using peach, join yarn in any htr along top. First bobble: 2ch, keep loops of 3htr on hook, yarn over and pull through all loops on hook. *2ch, miss 2, bobble of 4htr, rep from * along top edge. In 3 corners: (2ch, bobble of 4htr) 3 times. Along 2 sides: **1ch, miss 2, bobble of 4htr, rep from ** along each side. 2ch, close with sl st in top of first bobble.

NOTE: If this doesn't match exactly to 'miss 2, bobble' rhythm, just work a 'miss 3' or 'miss 1' bobble for this closing. Fasten off and weave in ends.

Using dark blue, join in yarn with sl st in any 2ch sp along top. 2ch, 1tr, 2ch, sl st in top of tr, 1htr, 1dc in top of bobble. *In next 2ch sp of previous row: 1htr, 1tr, 2ch, sl st in top of tr, 1htr, 1dc in top of next bobble. Rep from * along top edge and corners. Along 2 sides: **in next 1ch sp of previous row: 1htr, 2ch, sl st in top of htr, 1htr, 1dc in top of next bobble. Rep from ** along each side. End with 1htr and sl st in top of first tr. Fasten off and weave in ends.

Striped baby blanket

The perfect striped blanket with cute edging – use your favourite colours to create an heirloom piece as you dream about your baby.

Yarn:
DK weight
50% wool/50% cotton
(100 m/109 yd, 50 g/1¾ oz)

- 2 balls pale grey
- 4 balls ecru
- 2 balls green
- 2 balls yellow
- 1 ball blue

Hook: 4 mm (US G-6)

Tension: 16 sts x 9 rows = 10 cm (4 in) square over tr

Size: 58.5 cm x 84 cm (23 in x 33 in)

To make the blanket

Using pale grey, loosely work 91ch.

Row 1: Starting in third ch from hook, 89tr.

Rows 2–6: Work 6 rows of turn, 2ch (counts as st here and throughout), 89tr. Fasten off.

Rows 7 and 8: Using ecru, work 2 rows of turn, 2ch, 89tr. Fasten off.

Rows 9–14: Using green, work 6 rows of turn, 2ch, 89tr. Fasten off.

Rows 15 and 16: Using ecru, work 2 rows of turn, 2ch, 89tr. Fasten off.

Rows 17–22: Using yellow, work 6 rows of turn, 2ch, 89tr. Fasten off.

Rows 23 and 24: Using ecru, work 2 rows of turn, 2ch, 89tr. Fasten off.

Rows 25–30: Using blue, work 6 rows of turn, 2ch, 89tr. Fasten off.

Rows 31 and 32: Using ecru, work 2 rows of turn, 2ch, 89tr. Fasten off.

Rows 33–38: Using pale grey, work 6 rows of turn, 2ch, 89tr. Fasten off.

Rows 39 and 40: Using ecru, work 2 rows of turn, 2ch, 89tr. Fasten off.

Rows 41–44: Using yellow, work 4 rows of turn, 2ch, 89tr. Fasten off.

Rows 45 and 46: Using ecru, work 2 rows of turn, 2ch, 89tr. Fasten off.

Rows 47–50: Using green, work 4 rows of turn, 2ch, 89tr. Fasten off.

Rows 51 and 52: Using ecru, work 2 rows of turn, 2ch, 89tr. Fasten off.

Rows 53–56: Using pale grey, work 4 rows of turn, 2ch, 89tr. Fasten off.

Rows 57 and 58: Using ecru, work 2 rows of turn, 2ch, 89tr. Fasten off.

Rows 59–62: Using blue, work 4 rows of turn, 2ch, 89tr. Fasten off.

Rows 63 and 64: Using ecru, work 2 rows of turn, 2ch, 89tr. Fasten off.

Rows 65 and 66: Using yellow, work 2 rows of turn, 2ch, 89tr. Fasten off.

Rows 67 and 68: Using ecru, work 2 rows of turn, 2ch, 89tr. Fasten off.

Rows 69 and 70: Using pale grey, work 2 rows of turn, 2ch, 89tr. Fasten off.

Rows 71 and 72: Using ecru, work 2 rows of turn, 2ch, 89tr. Fasten off.

Rows 73 and 74: Using green, work 2 rows of turn, 2ch, 89tr. Fasten off.

Edging

Join in ecru yarn in any st along top row with sl st.

Round 1: 1ch, 1htr in every st. Corners: 3htr. Sides: 2htr in every row end. Close with sl st in first htr.

Round 2: 1ch, *1dc, 2ch, miss 2, rep from * all around. Corners: miss 1 or miss none, depending on what gives you a nice rounded corner that doesn't pull up. Close with sl st in first dc. Fasten off.

Round 3: Using yellow, join yarn with sl st in any 2ch sp. 1ch, *2htr around 2ch sp, 1ch, rep from * all around. Close with sl st in first htr. Fasten off.

Round 4: Using ecru, join yarn with sl st in any 1ch sp. 1ch, *1dc around 1ch sp, 3ch. Rep from * all around. Corners: 4ch between dc sts. Close with sl st in first dc. Fasten off and weave in all ends.

Pastel waves nursery cushion

Add colour to the nursery with an eye-catching cushion that brings a little comfort to those nighttime feeds. It matches beautifully with the shawl on page 45.

Yarn:
Aran weight
55% wool/33% acrylic/
12% cashmere
(90 m/98 yd, 50 g/1¾ oz)
• 1 ball each pale green; aqua blue, dark blue; dark purple; heather; pale lilac; peach; coral pink

Hook: 5 mm (US H-8)

Notions: 3 buttons approx. 2 cm (¾ in) wide, safety pins, pillow insert

Tension: 16 sts x 9 rows = 10 cm (4 in) square over wave pattern

Size: 44.5 cm x 44.5 cm (17½ in x 17½ in)

To make the cushion

Using pale green, work 53ch.

Row 1: Starting in third ch from hook, 51htr (52 sts).

Row 2: Turn, 1ch (does not count as st here and throughout), 52htr.

Row 3: Turn, 1ch, 1tr, *2dtr, 2tr, 2htr, 2dc, 2htr, 2tr. Rep from * 3 times. End with 2dtr and 1tr. Fasten off.

Row 4: Turn, join aqua blue in last dtr from row 3 (NOTE: This is not last st of row 3), 1ch, starting in same st with *2htr in each of next 2 sts, 3htr, (htr2tog) twice, 3htr. Rep from * 3 times. End with 2htr in each of next 2 sts and miss last st.

Row 5: Turn, miss first st, 1ch, *2htr in each of next 2 sts, 3htr, (htr2tog) twice, 3htr. Rep from * 3 times. End with 2htr in each of next 2 sts and miss last st. Fasten off.

Rep row 5 to make wave pattern and work colours in order they are given in the yarn list.

Work 2 rows in each of next 5 colours, starting with dark blue and ending with peach. Work 4 rows in coral pink.

Reverse order of colours and work 2 rows in each colour starting with peach and ending with pale green.

Continue working 2 rows of each colour, starting with pale green and ending with coral pink. Then reverse order again, starting with coral pink and ending with pale green.

Buttonhole row: Using pale green, turn, miss first st, 1ch, 2htr in each of next 2 sts, *3htr, (htr2tog) twice, 3htr, 1htr in next st, 2ch, 1htr in next st. Rep from * twice. End with 3htr, (htr2tog) twice, 3htr, 2htr in each of next 2 sts, miss last st.

Work 1 more row like row 5, working 4htr in each buttonhole loop.

Fasten off.

Assembly

Weave in ends carefully. Fold 2 ends into centre along rows of coral pink, matching colours at edges and with buttonholes on top. Pin together with safety pins to hold matching stripes tog. Turn cover so WS is facing you and st sides tog. Attach buttons securely (see page 92), or if you prefer, attach a hook-and-loop tape closure instead.

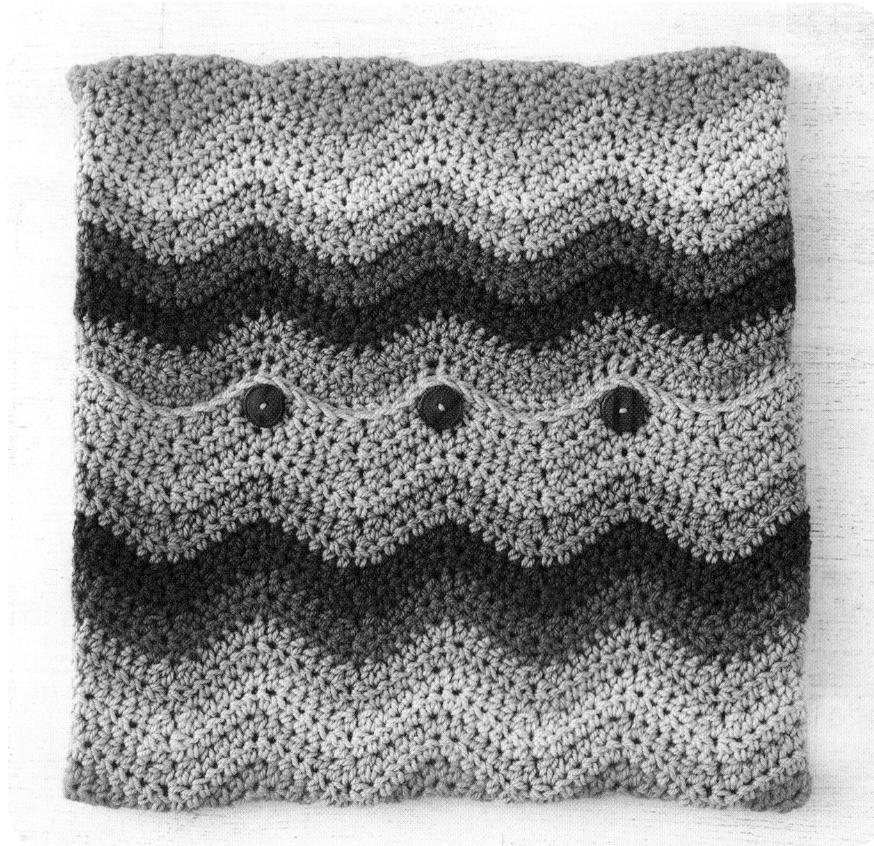

Larger cushion

To make a bigger cushion, add waves. The wave works on a stitch count of a multiple of 12 + 5. Every set of 12 stitches creates a wave.

Sleeveless cardigan

A cute, all season, sleeveless cardigan made with a soft cotton-wool blend can easily be adjusted to your favourite colour scheme.

Yarn:
DK weight
50% wool/50% cotton
(100 m/109 yd, 50 g/1¾ oz)
- 2 balls ecru
- 1 ball pale grey
- 1 ball green
- Scraps of yellow

Hook: 4 mm (US G-6)

Tension: 16 sts x 10 rows = 10 cm (4 in) square over tr and dc pattern

Size: 45.5 cm (18 in) chest, 24 cm (9½ in) length
Fits 3-month-old baby

Special stitches: Decorative stitch (see page 115)

To make the cardigan

The cardigan is worked in 1 piece from the top down. Using ecru, work 30ch.

Row 1: Starting in third ch from hook, 4tr, *2tr in next st, 2tr, rep from * 5 times. 2tr in next st, 5tr (36 sts).

Row 2: Turn, 2ch (counts as st here and throughout), 4tr, *2tr in next st, 3tr, rep from * 5 times. 2tr in next st, 6tr (43 sts). Fasten off.

Row 3: Using pale grey, turn, 2ch, 4tr, *2tr in next st, 4tr, rep from * 5 times. 2tr in next st, 7tr (50 sts).

Row 4: Turn, 2ch, 4tr, *2tr in next st, 5tr, rep from * 6 times. 2tr in next st, 2tr (58 sts). Fasten off.

Row 5: Using ecru, turn, 2ch, 4tr, *2tr in next st, 6tr, rep from * 6 times. 2tr in next st, 3tr (66 sts).

Row 6: Turn, 2ch, 4tr, *2tr in next st, 7tr, rep from * 6 times. 2tr in next st, 4tr (74 sts). Fasten off.

Row 7: Using pale green, turn, 2ch, 8tr, *2tr in next st, 8tr, rep from * 6 times. 2tr in next st, 1tr (82 sts).

Row 8: Turn, 2ch, 5tr, *2tr in next st, 9tr, rep from * 6 times. 2tr in next st, 5tr (90 sts). Fasten off.

Row 9: Using ecru, turn, 2ch, 8tr, *2tr in next st, 10tr, rep from * 6 times. 2tr in next st, 3tr (98 sts).

Row 10: Turn, 2ch, 8tr, 2tr in next st, 25tr, 2tr in next st, 7tr, 2tr in next st, 4tr, 2tr in next st, 8tr, 2tr in next st, 33tr, 2tr in next st, 6tr (104 sts).

Row 11: In this row you'll create armholes by missing sts. Turn, 2ch, 15tr, 5ch, miss 18, 36tr, 5ch, miss 18, 16tr (68tr + 10 ch = 78 sts).

Row 12: Turn, 1ch, 77dc.

Row 13: Turn, ch 3, 77dtr.

Rows 14–22: Alternate rows 12 and 13 four times. End with 1 row of dc as for row 12. Fasten off and weave in ends.

Yellow stripes and ties

Using yellow yarn, work 20ch, insert hook in first st of row 1 and, with yarn at back, work decorative row of sl st in top of all sts of row 1. 20ch and weave in ends. Do the same for rows 5 and 9.

Snuggly cowl and hat

Keep your little one's head and neck warm with this stylish little bobble cowl and hat combo.

Yarn:
2 ply weight
100% wool
(85 m/93 yd, 25 g/1 oz)
- 1 ball red
- 1 ball purple
- 1 ball peach

Hook: 3.5 mm (US E-4)

Tension: 8 bobbles x 10 rows = 10 cm (4 in) square over bobble pattern

Size: 73.5 cm (29 in) circumference, 5 cm (2 in) width
Fits 6-month-old baby

Special stitches: dc foundation chain (see page 109)
Bobbles of 2htr and 3htr (see page 111)

To make the cowl

Using red, make a dc foundation ch of 120. Close with sl st in first dc, making sure ch is not twisted.

Round 1: 2ch, bobble of 2htr, 2ch, miss 1. *Bobble of 3htr, 2ch, miss bobble, rep from * all around. Close with sl st in top of first bobble. Fasten off and weave in ends.

Round 2: Using peach, join in yarn in any 2ch sp of round 1. 2ch, bobble of 2htr, 2ch, miss 1. *Bobble of 3htr, 2ch, miss 1, rep from * all around. Close with sl st in top of first bobble. Fasten off and weave in ends.

Round 3: Using purple, join in yarn in any 2ch sp of round 2. 2ch, bobble of 2htr, 2ch, miss bobble. *Bobble of 3htr, 2ch, miss 1, rep from * all around. Close with sl st in top of first bobble. Fasten off and weave in ends.

Round 4: Using red, join in yarn in any 2ch sp of round 3. 2ch, bobble of 2htr, 1ch, miss bobble. *Bobble of 3htr, 1ch, miss 1, rep from * all around. Close with sl st in top of first bobble. Fasten off and weave in ends.

Round 5: Rotate so that bottom red row is now at top. Using purple, join in yarn in any 2ch sp of round 1. 2ch, bobble of 2htr, 1ch, miss bobble. *Bobble of 3htr, 1ch, miss 1, rep from * all around. Close with sl st in top of first bobble. Fasten off and weave in ends.

Yarn:
2 ply weight
100% wool
(93 yd/85 m, 1 oz/25 g)
- 1 ball red
- 1 ball purple
- 1 ball peach

Hook: 3.5 mm (US E-4)

Tension: 8 bobbles x 10 rows = 10 cm (4 in) square over bobble pattern

Size: 43 cm (17 in) circumference, 14 cm (5½ in) length
Fits 6-month-old baby

Special stitches: Bobbles of 2htr and 3htr (see page 111)

To make the hat

Using red, work 3ch and close into a circle with sl st.

Round 1: 1ch, 6dc in circle.

Round 2: 2ch, bobble of 2htr in first dc, 3ch. *Bobble of 3htr in next dc, 3ch, rep from * 4 times. Close with sl st in top of first bobble. (Total of 6 bobbles in this round.)

Round 3: 1dc in next 3ch sp, 2ch, bobble of 2htr, 2ch, bobble of 3htr, 2ch. *In next loop: Bobble of 3htr, 2ch, bobble of 3htr, 2ch, rep from * 4 times. Close with sl st in top of first bobble. (Total of 12 bobbles in this round.)

Round 4: 1dc in next 2ch sp, 2ch, bobble of 2htr, 2ch. *In next loop: Bobble of 3htr, 2ch, bobble of 3htr, 2ch. In next loop: Bobble of 3htr, 2ch, rep from * 4 times. In next loop: Bobble of 3htr, 2ch, bobble of 3htr, 2ch. Close with sl st in top of first bobble. (Total of 18 bobbles in this round.)

Round 5: 1dc in next 2ch sp, 2ch, bobble of 2htr, 2ch, bobble of 3htr, 2ch. *In next loop: Bobble, 2ch. In next loop: Bobble, 2ch, bobble, 2ch. In next loop: Bobble, 2ch, bobble, 2ch, rep from * 4 times. In next loop: Bobble, 2ch. In next loop: Bobble, 2ch, bobble, 2ch. Close with sl st in top of first bobble.

Round 6: 1dc in next 2ch sp, 2ch, bobble of 2htr, 2ch. *In next loop: Bobble of 3htr, rep from * all around. 2ch, close with sl st in top of first bobble.

Rounds 7–11: Work 6 rounds of 30 bobbles. Fasten off and weave in ends.

Round 12: Using peach, work 1 round of 30 bobbles. Fasten off and weave in ends.

Rounds 13 and 14: Using purple, work 2 rounds of 30 bobbles. For last round, 1ch between bobbles. Fasten off and weave in ends.

Round 15: Using red, work 1 round of bobbles and 1ch. Fasten off and weave in ends.

For a larger hat

For a larger hat size, add 1 more round of increases:

Round 6: 1dc in next 2ch sp, 2ch, bobble of 2htr, 2ch. (Bobble of 3htr, 2ch) 3 times. In next loop: Bobble, 2ch, bobble, 2ch. *(Bobble, 2ch)

4 times. In next loop: Bobble, 2ch, bobble, 2ch, rep from * 3 times. Close with sl st in top of first bobble. (Total of 36 bobbles in this round.)

Now cont making rounds of 36 bobbles and do a couple more than original pattern says, until you've reached desired length.

Flower for hat

Using peach, work 3ch. Close into a circle with sl st.

Round 1: 1ch, 6dc in ring. Close with sl st in first dc.

Round 2: 1ch, *bobble of 4htr, 2ch, rep from * 5 times. Close with sl st in top of first bobble. Fasten off and weave in ends.

Round 3: Using purple, join yarn with sl st in any 2ch sp. 1ch, 3htr in same loop. *Sl st in top of bobble, 4htr in next loop, rep from * 4 times. Sl st in top of next bobble, 1htr in loop where you started. Close with sl st in first htr. Fasten off and weave in ends.

Assembly

Using red, attach flower to hat, stitching through middle of flower and around back of flower petals.

Rattle buddy

Soft and squeezy, this rattle is sure to be your baby's favourite toy. The size and shape will make it easy for your little one to grab and shake.

Yarn:
DK weight
50% wool/50% cotton
(100 m/109 yd, 50 g/1¾ oz)
- 1 ball ecru
- 1 ball pale grey
- Scraps of yellow and blue

Hook: 4 mm (US G-6)

Notions: Wadding for stuffing, safety rattle

Tension: 22 sts x 20 rows = 10 cm (4 in) square over tr

Size: 16 cm (6¼ in) height, 13.5 cm (5¼ in) arm width

Body

Using ecru, work 3ch. Close into a circle with sl st.

Round 1: 1ch, 6dc in circle. Close with sl st in first dc (6 sts).

Round 2: 1ch, 2dc in every st. Close with sl st in first dc (12 sts).

Round 3: 1ch, *1dc, 2dc in next st, rep from * all around. Close with sl st in first dc (18 sts).

Round 4: 1ch, *2dc, 2dc in next st, rep from * all around. Close with sl st in first dc (24 sts).

Round 5: 1ch, *3dc, 2dc in next st, rep from * all around. Close with sl st in first dc (30 sts).

Round 6: 1ch, *4dc, 2dc in next st, rep from * all around. Close with sl st in first dc (36 sts).

Round 7: 1ch, *5dc, 2dc in next st, rep from * all around. Close with sl st in first dc (42 sts).

Rounds 8 and 9: 1ch, dc all around. Close with sl st in first dc (42 sts). Fasten off.

Round 10: Using blue, 1ch, dc all around. Close with sl st in first dc. Fasten off.

Round 11: Using pale grey, 1ch, dc all around. Close with sl st in first dc.

Round 12: 1ch, *5dc, dc2tog, rep from * all around. Close with sl st in first dc (36 sts).

Round 13: 1ch, dc all around. Close with sl st in first dc (36 sts).

Round 14: 1ch, *4dc, dc2tog, rep from * all around. Close with sl st in first dc (30 sts).

Round 15: 1ch, dc all around. Close with sl st in first dc (30 sts).

Round 16: 1ch, *3dc, dc2tog, rep from * all around. Close with sl st in first dc (24 sts).

Rounds 17–20: Work 4 rounds of 1ch, dc all around. Close with sl st in first dc (24 sts).

Round 21: 1ch, *2dc, dc2tog, rep from * all around. Close with sl st in first dc (18 sts).

Rounds 22–24: Work 3 rounds of 1ch, dc all around. Close with sl st in first dc (18 sts). Fasten off and weave in ends.

Collar

Using yellow look at body from top down, join yarn in front middle of top round. 1ch, 18dc in outside loops of sts. Close with sl st in first dc. Turn, 2ch, 3tr in first st, miss 2, 12dc, miss 2, 3tr in last st, 2ch. Close with sl st in same st. Fasten off and weave in ends.

Arms

Using ecru, work 3ch. Close into a circle with sl st.

Round 1: 1ch, 6dc in circle. Close with sl st in first dc (6 sts).

Round 2: 1ch, 2dc in every st. Close with sl st in first dc (12 sts). Fasten off.

Round 3: Using blue, 1ch, 12dc. Close with sl st in first dc. Fasten off.

Round 4: Using pale grey, 1ch, 12dc, don't close. Weave in ends of previous rows.

Rounds 5–13: 9 rounds of 12dc. Work in continuous rounds in spiral style by not closing with a sl st at end of each round. Stuff arms lightly and flatten tops. Attach to body, directly beneath collar, by working 5dc through both thicknesses of arm and into dc on body. Miss 4dc and attach second arm in same way.

Head

Work as for body using ecru until round 6 (36 sts).

Rounds 7–12: Work 5 rounds of 36 sts. 1ch, dc all around. Close with sl st in first dc.

Round 13: As round 14 of body.

Round 14: As round 16 of body.

Round 15: As round 21 of body (18 sts).

Fasten off and leave a long yarn end for sewing up. Stuff head lightly, just for shaping. Using dark-coloured yarn, embroider a face onto head.

Ears (make 2)

Using ecru, work 3ch. Close into a circle with sl st.

Row 1: 1ch, 3dc in circle.

Row 2: Turn, 1ch, 2dc in every st (6 sts).

Row 3: Turn, 1ch, *2dc in next st, 1dc, rep from * twice. Close with sl st in first dc at beg of row (9 sts). Fasten off, leaving a long end for sewing up.

Assembly

Using long yarn ends, sew an ear to each side of head. Remove stuffing, weave in ends, and replace stuffing, this time stuffing fully. With long yarn end left at head, attach head to body into back loop of sts you didn't use when attaching collar.

Soft baby bonnet

A beautiful, soft bonnet is perfect for those precious first weeks with your newborn. It's easily adjusted to a boy's or girl's colour scheme, or you could keep it gender neutral with white.

Yarn:
1 ply weight
100% extra fine merino
(390 m/427 yd, 50 g/1¾ oz)
- 1 ball white
- 1 ball acid yellow

Hook: 2.75 mm (US C-2)

Tension: 10 x 3 tr clusters x 11 rows = 10 cm (4 in) square over granny square rounds

Size: 26 cm (10¼ in) wide, 13.5 cm (5¼ in) long
Fits a newborn baby

First half of bonnet

Using white, crochet a seven round granny square (see page 114). Turn after every round. This affects how you work the pattern in the corner where rounds start and end. After closing round 1 with a sl st in second beg ch, 1dc in corner, turn. 3ch, 3tr in same corner. Cont round as usual. Close rounds with 2tr in corner and a sl st in second beg ch. Rep like this for a total of 7 rounds.

Round 8: Work as previous 7 rounds, but in third corner, make 6tr instead of 3tr, 2ch, 3tr.

Round 9: Work as previous rounds, but in first corner make 3tr between third and fourth tr. Cont round as usual.

Round 10: Work round as usual, working only 3 corners.

Row 11: DON'T turn, 2ch, 1tr in corner. Work 3tr clusters around 2 sides and rounded corner in middle. End with 2tr in last corner.

Row 12: Turn, 2ch, 3tr after last 2tr of row 11. Work 3tr clusters around 2 sides and rounded corner to end. End with 1tr between 2tr of row 11.

Row 13: Turn, 2ch, 1tr before last 3tr cluster of row 12. Work 3tr clusters around 2 sides and rounded corner to end. End 2tr in space between last 3tr cluster of round 12 and last 2ch. Fasten off and weave in ends.

Second half of bonnet

Work as for first half of bonnet, but on round 8, work flat corner of 6tr in first corner instead of third. On round 9, flat corner will be third corner.

Don't fasten off when second half is completed.

Take first half and hold tog with second half, matching flat corners. Join tog, matching st to st, by working dc through both inside loops of sts. Fasten off and weave in ends.

Edging

Using acid yellow, start at bottom of bonnet.

Round 1: Join yarn with sl st in a tr. 1ch, dc all around neck and face line. Corners: 1dc, 2ch, 1dc in 2ch sp. Row ends from rows 11–13: 1dc per row end on neck; 2dc per row end on forehead. Close with sl st in first dc.

Round 2: 1ch, 1dc in every st all around. Corners: 3dc in 2ch sp. Close with sl st in first dc.

Row 3: 1ch, 1dc in every st all around. Corners: 3dc in middle dc of 3dc corner of row 2. Close with sl st in first dc. Fasten off and weave in ends.

Straps

At bottom front, join yarn in last st with sl st. 1ch, 2dc. Work about 60 rows – or 15 cm (6 in) – of 1ch, 2dc, turn. Fasten off and weave in ends. Starting at side of strap, which is attached to bonnet, work 1dc in every row end around entire strap. End with a sl st back in bonnet edge. Fasten off and weave in ends. Rep on other side of bonnet.

Larger sizes

For toddler-sized bonnets, use a thicker yarn and matching hook. For example, 4 ply weight and 3.5 mm (US E-4) hook, or even DK weight and 4 mm (US G-6) hook, depending on your tension.

Nautical coat hangers

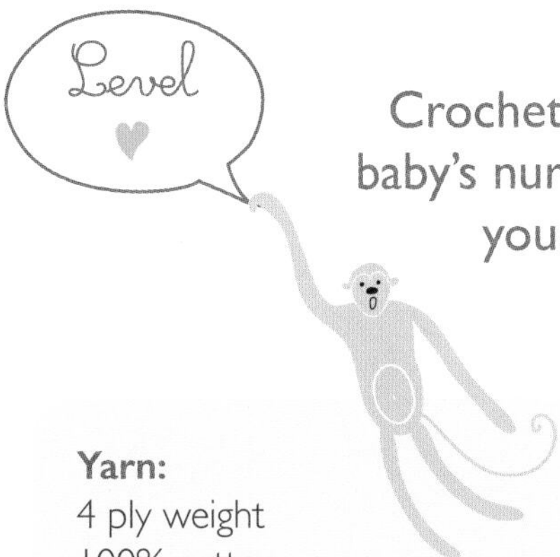

Crocheted coat hangers add the finishing touch to your baby's nursery wardrobe. Make them in colours that match your handmade cardigans for an adorable look.

Yarn:
4 ply weight
100% cotton
(125 m/137 yd, 50 g/1¾ oz)
- 1 ball red
- 1 ball white
- 1 ball baby blue
- 1 ball royal blue
- 1 ball pale green

Hook: 3 mm (US D-3)

Notions: 3 coat hangers

Tension: 20 sts x 12 rows = 10 cm (4 in) square over htr

Size: To fit 26.5 cm (10½ in) wide coat hangers

Red-and-white hanger with blue bow

Using red, work 12ch.

Row 1: Starting in second ch from hook, 11htr.

Rows 2–10: Turn, 2ch (does not count as a st here and throughout), 11htr.

Row 11: Using white, turn and join with sl st. 2ch, 11htr in back loop of every st.

Rows 12–24: Turn, 2ch, 11htr.

Row 25: Turn, join red with sl st, 2ch, 11htr in back loop of every st.

Rows 26–34: Turn, 2ch, 11htr. Fasten off and weave in ends.

Easy assembly

Leave longer yarn ends at the beginning and end of a new colour, so that you can use them to sew the hanger cover together.

Bow

Using baby blue, work 51ch.

Row 1: Starting in second ch from hook, 50dc.

Weave in ends. Fold into a bow shape and sew to middle of crochet hanger cover, on lower half, using matching yarn. Weave in ends tightly at back.

Assembly
Using red, sew ends closed. Insert coat hanger hook in middle of work and, using matching yarn colours, close bottom. The crochet cover should be nice and tight.

Navy-and-white hanger with red bow
Using royal blue, work 12ch.

Row 1: Starting in second ch from hook, 11htr.

Row 2: Turn, 2ch, 11htr. Fasten off.

Row 3: Turn, join white with sl st, 1ch, 11htr.

Row 4: Turn, 2ch, 11htr. Fasten off.

Rows 5–34: Rep rows 3 and 4, alternating royal blue and white (9 royal blue stripes and 8 white ones).

Bow
Using red, work 7ch.

Row 1: Starting in third ch from hook, 6dc.

Rows 2–24: Turn, 1ch, 6dc.

Using red, sew ends together to form a loop. Weave in ends and position in middle of crochet hanger cover, on lower half. Stitch in place, sewing over bow several times to bind it in middle.

Assembly
Assemble as for red-and-white hanger with blue bow.

White, blue and green striped hanger
Using baby blue, work 12ch.

Row 1: Starting in second ch from hook, 11htr.

Rows 2 and 3: Turn, 2ch, 11htr. Fasten off.

Rows 4 and 5: Using white, turn, 2ch, 11htr. Fasten off.

Rows 6 and 7: Using pale green, turn, 2ch, 11htr. Fasten off.

Rows 8 and 9: Using white, turn, 2ch, 11htr. Fasten off.

Rows 10–12: Using baby blue, turn, 2ch, 11htr. Fasten off.

Rows 13–22: Using white, turn, 2ch, 11htr. Fasten off.

Rows 23–25: Using baby blue, turn, 2ch, 11htr. Fasten off.

Rows 26 and 27: Using white, turn, 2ch, 11htr. Fasten off.

Rows 28 and 29: Using pale green, turn, 2ch, 11htr. Fasten off.

Rows 30 and 31: Using white, turn, 2ch, 11htr. Fasten off.

Rows 32–34: Using baby blue, turn, 2ch, 11htr. Fasten off.

Bow
Using royal blue, work 81ch.

Row 1: Starting in second ch from hook, 80dc.

Row 2: Turn, 1ch, 80dc. Fasten off and weave in ends.

Fold like a butterfly. Using royal blue, sew ends closed at back. Place in middle of crochet hanger cover, on lower half. Stitch in place, sewing over bow several times to bind it in middle.

Assembly
Assemble as for red-and-white hanger with blue bow.

Chapter Three

THE THIRD TRIMESTER

The waiting is nearly over, and in this section you'll find a charming selection of crochet projects to keep you busy during your third trimester. Focusing on small projects in preparation for the first few months with your newborn, you can choose from baby clothing and accessories, such as cute booties, sweaters, skirts and shorts, or why not put the finishing touches to the nursery with an adorable hanging sheep mobile?

Two tone baby booties

Cute little woollen booties keep small feet nice and warm. Fold the cuffs up or down for different looks.

Yarn:
4 ply weight
55% wool/33% acrylic/
12% cashmere
(125 m/137 yd, 50 g/1¾ oz)
- 1 ball light blue
- 1 ball teal

Hook: 3.5 mm (US E-4)

Tension: 22 sts × 14 rows = 10 cm (4 in) square over htr

Size: Sole 9 cm (3½ in) long, 4 cm (1½ in) wide
Fit 3-month-old baby

Special stitches: fptr (see page 117)
Back loop (see page 118)

To make the cuff

Using light blue, work 11ch.

Row 1: Starting in third ch from hook, 9tr.

Rows 2–16: Turn, 2ch, 9fptr. Close this strip of 16 rows into a circle by working sl st in sts of last row and around posts of first row sts. Don't fasten off. Cont with upper part of shoe.

To make the shoe body

Round 1: 1ch, 1htr in every row end. Close with sl st in first htr (16htr).

Round 2: 1ch, 16htr. Close with sl st in first htr.

Round 3: 1ch, 6htr, (2tr in next htr) 4 times, 6htr. Close with sl st in first htr (20 sts).

Round 4: 1ch, 8htr, (2tr in next htr) 4 times, 8htr. Close with sl st in first htr (24 sts).

Round 5: 1ch, 10htr, (2tr in next htr) 4 times, 10htr. Close with sl st in first htr (28 sts).

Round 6: 1ch, 12htr, (2tr in next htr) 4 times, 12htr. Close with sl st in first htr (32 sts).

Round 7: 1ch, 14htr, (2tr in next htr) 4 times, 14htr. Close with sl st in first htr (36 sts). Fasten off and weave in ends.

To make the sole

Using teal, work 9ch.

Round 1: 2dc in second ch from hook, 6dc, 4dc in last st. Cont to work back along same ch row in round: 6dc, 2dc in first st. Close with sl st in first dc.

Round 2: 1ch, 3htr in first st, 8dc, (3htr in next st) twice, 8dc, 3htr in last st. Close with sl st in first htr.

Round 3: 2ch, (2tr in next st) twice, 10htr, (2tr in next st) 4 times, 10htr, (2tr in next st) twice. Close with sl st in first tr. Don't fasten off.

Assembly

Working on WS of both parts, crochet upper and sole tog by working dc in both outside loops of sts. As an anchor, connect toe part first to make sure you're following same sts on sole and shoe. Weave in ends and turn bootie inside out. Now make other bootie in same way.

Striped baby beanie

Top it off with cuteness! A warm beanie hat accented with simple stripes to match the sweater and shorts on pages 89 and 87, respectively.

Yarn:
4 ply weight
55% wool/33% acrylic/
12% cashmere
(125 m/137 yd, 50 g/1¾ oz)
- 1 ball teal
- 1 ball light blue

Hook: 3.5 mm (US E-4)

Tension: 18 sts x 10 rows = 10 cm (4 in) square over tr

Size: Approx. 28 cm (11 in) circumference, 16.5 cm (6½ in) length
Fits 3- to 6-month-old baby

Special stitches: bptr (see page 117)
Back loop (see page 118)

To make the beanie

Using teal, work 9ch.

Row 1: Starting in third ch from hook, 8tr.

Row 2 (WS): Turn, 2ch (counts as 1tr), 7bptr.

Row 3 (RS): Turn, 2ch (counts as 1tr), 7tr.

Rep rows 2 and 3, alternating between them, until you have 34 rows (17 ribs on WS).

Join the strip

Close into a circle by matching ends with RS tog. Work 8dc in sts of last row and first row on WS. Fasten off and weave in ends.

Crown of beanie

On side where you started join, with ribs facing out, join in teal yarn in any row end with sl st and 2ch. 1tr in that same row end, 2tr in every row end all around. End with 1tr in row end where you started, close with sl st in first tr. You now have a circle of 68tr.

Round 2: 2ch, 68tr. Using light blue, close with sl st in first tr. Cut teal yarn.

Round 3: Using light blue, 2ch, 68tr in back loop of sts. Using teal, close with sl st in first tr. Cut light blue yarn.

Round 4: Using teal, 2ch, 68tr in back loop of sts. Using light blue, close with sl st in first tr. Cut teal yarn.

Round 5: Using light blue, 2ch, 68tr in back loop of sts. Using teal, close with sl st in first tr. Cut light blue yarn.

Round 6: Using teal, 2ch, 68tr in back loop of sts. Close with sl st in first tr.

Rounds 7–10: Work 4 rows of 2ch, 68tr. Close with sl st in first tr.

Round 11: 2ch, *2tr, tr2tog, rep from * all around (51 sts). Close with sl st in first tr.

Round 12: 2ch, *tr2tog, 1tr, rep from * all around (34 sts). Close with sl st in first tr2tog.

Rounds 13 and 14: Work 2 rows of 2ch, 34tr. Close with sl st in first tr.

Close top of hat

To close top of hat, fold first 4 sts alongside last 4 sts and, using teal, work 4dc in inner loops of both sets of sts. Fold next 8 sts in half and work 4dc in same way to close. Fasten off. Fold next 8 sts in half, join teal, and make another 4dc in same way through both sets of sts, and again in next 8 sts folded tog. Fasten off and weave in ends.

Chunky beanie

To make a larger beanie, add 2 or 3 rows to the beginning, before starting the 'Crown of Beanie' section and add 3 or 4 rows to rounds 7–10.

Drawstring baby skirt

Coordinate a sweet skirt with the short sleeved sweater on page 89 to make a great outfit for your cute little addition to the family.

Yarn:
4 ply weight
55% wool/ 33% acrylic/
12% cashmere
(125 m/137 yd, 50 g/1¾ oz)
- 2 balls coral pink
- 1 ball dark blue

Hook: 3.5 mm (US E-4)

Tension: 18 sts x 10 rows = 10 cm (4 in) square over tr

Size: Approx. 49.5 cm (19½ in) hem, 35.5 cm (14 in) waist, 18 cm (7 in) length
Fits 3- to 6-month-old baby

Special stitches: dc foundation chain (see page 109)
Reverse dc (see page 110)
Back loop (see page 118)

To make the skirt

Using coral pink, make a dc foundation ch of 60 sts and close into a circle with sl st, making sure NOT to twist ch.

Rounds 1 and 2: Work 2 rounds of 2ch, 60htr. Close with sl st in first htr.

Round 3: 2ch, *2htr, 1ch, miss 1, rep from * 19 times. Close with sl st in first htr.

Round 4: 2ch, 1htr in every st and around every 1ch sp of round 3 (60htr). Close with sl st in first htr.

Round 5: 2ch, 60htr, close with sl st in first htr.

Round 6: 2ch, *working in back loop of sts: 1tr, 2tr in next st, rep from * all around (90tr). Close with sl st in first tr.

Rounds 7–20: Work 14 rows of 2ch, 90tr. Close with sl st in first tr.

Round 21: 1ch, work 90 reverse dc.

Using dark blue, make dc foundation ch of 90 sts and weave through holes of row 3 to be able to tighten waist a little.

Adjustments

To make the skirt longer or shorter, you can easily add or omit a couple of rounds of 90tr (rounds 7–20). To make the skirt wider, add stitches to the base row in groups of 3.

Safety first!

Wooden beads can be a choking hazard so make sure you attach them securely. Alternatively, why not try using hook-and-loop tape as a baby safe fastening.

Colourful bandana bibs

Keep baby's clothes clean adorably. Bandana bibs are the perfect quick project and they're small enough to pop into any bag for an outing.

Yarn:
2 ply weight
100% cotton
(92 m/101 yd, 25 g/1 oz)
• 1 ball each main colours: red, yellow, apple green, navy
• 1 ball white

Hook: 3.25 mm (US D-3)

Notions: 1 wooden bead button per bib

Tension: 26 sts x 19 rows = 10 cm (4 in) square over htr

Size: 12.5 cm x 28 cm (5 in x 11 in) at widest point

Special stitches: Decorative stitch (see page 115)

To make the bibs

Using main colour, work 3ch.

Row 1: Work 3tr in first ch.

Row 2: Turn, 2ch, 3htr in first st, 1htr, 3htr in last st.

Row 3: Turn, 2ch, 2htr in first st, 1htr in every st to last st, 2htr in last st.

Rows 4–20: Rep rows 2 and 3 eight times and end with a row 2 (61 sts).

Rows 21–23: Rep row 3 three times (67 sts).

Don't fasten off. Cont around bottom of triangle as follows: 2dc in every row end around bottom, 3dc in bottom point. Close with sl st in first htr of row 23. Fasten off.

Edging

Join white in last st, 2ch, work along top of triangle as follows: 15htr, (htr2tog) 6 times, 12htr, (htr2tog) 6 times, 15htr. In corner: 1htr, ch 5 (or more to make larger buttonhole loop), 1htr in same corner. Work 1htr in every st around bottom of triangle, 3htr in bottom point. In st where you began: 2htr and close with sl st in first dc. Fasten off, leaving a long end of yarn to securely attach wooden bead.

Decoration

Work all decorations using white. On red bib, work decorative row of sl st, 3 rows at bottom from white edge to white edge. On yellow bib, embroider a sun motif; on apple green bib, a leaf motif; and on navy bib, a flower.

Cute baby shorts

Adorable shorts allow extra room for that nappy-covered bottom. They work perfectly with bare legs in summer or with tights in cooler weather.

Yarn:
4 ply weight
55% wool/33% acrylic/
12% cashmere
(125 m/137 yd, 50 g/1¾ oz)
- 2 balls teal
- 1 ball light blue

Hook: 3.5 mm (US E-4)

Tension: 18 sts x 10 rows = 10 cm (4 in) square over tr

Size: Approx. 25.5 cm (14 in) waist
Fits 3- to 6-month-old baby

Special stitches: dc foundation ch (see page 109)
Reverse dc (see page 110)
Back loop (see page 118)

To make the shorts

Using teal, make a dc foundation ch of 60 sts and close into a circle with sl st, making sure NOT to twist the ch.

Rounds 1 and 2: Work 2 rounds of 2ch, 60htr. Close with sl st in first htr.

Round 3: 2ch, *2htr, 1ch, miss 1, rep from * 19 times. Close with sl st in first htr.

Round 4: 2ch, 1htr in every st and around every 1ch sp of round 3 (60htr). Close with sl st in first htr.

Round 5: 2ch, 60htr, close with sl st in first htr.

Round 6: 2ch, *working in back loop of sts: 1htr, 2htr in next st, rep from * all around (90htr). Close with sl st in first htr.

Round 7: To make more room for a nappy at the back, divide 90 sts into dc and tr as follows: 2ch, 43tr, 1htr, 45dc, 1htr. Close with sl st in first tr. If you prefer, you can add st markers at end and beg of tr part.

Round 8: 2ch, 90tr. Close with sl st in first tr.

Rounds 9–16: Rep rounds 7–8 four times. Leave markers in. Fasten off and weave in ends.

Crotch

Facing front of shorts, counting from st markers, join yarn with sl st in 16th st, 2ch, 12tr. Work 6 rows of turn, 2ch, 12tr. Counting same 18 sts at back, attach crotch with sl st in inside loops of 12 sts. Fasten off and weave in ends.

Around the leg holes

Join yarn with sl st in any tr around back.

Row 1: 2ch, *1htr, htr2tog, rep from * all around, except for sides of crotch part: make 2htr in every row end. Close with sl st in first htr.

Row 2: 2ch, *2htr, htr2tog, rep from * all around. Close with sl st in first htr.

Row 3: 2ch, 1htr in every st all around. Close with sl st in first htr.

Row 4: 1ch, work reverse dc in every st all around. Fasten off and weave in ends.

Using light blue, make a dc foundation ch of 90 sts and weave through holes of row 3. This will allow you to tighten the waist a little.

Complementary baby sweaters

Infant sweaters are quick to crochet; make a short sleeved version for summer and one with long sleeves for the cooler months.

Yarn:
4 ply weight
55% wool/33% acrylic/
12% cashmere
(125 m/137 yd, 50 g/1¾ oz)
- 2 balls dark blue
- 1 balls coral pink

Hook: 3.5 mm (US E-4)

Notions: 3 buttons, approx. 1.5 cm (⅝ in) wide

Tension: 18 sts x 10 rows = 10 cm (4 in) square over tr

Size: 44.5 cm (17½ in) chest,
20.5 cm (8 in) length
Fits 0- to 3-month-old baby

Special stitches: dc foundation ch (see page 109)
Reverse dc (see page 110)
Back loop (see page 118)

To make the short sleeved sweater

Using dark blue, make a dc foundation ch of 48 sts.

Row 1: 2ch (does not count as a st here and throughout), 48htr.

Row 2: Turn, 2ch, 7htr, (2htr in next st) twice, 6htr, (2htr in next st) twice, 14htr, (2htr in next st) twice, 6htr, (2htr in next st) twice, 7htr (56 sts).

Row 3: Turn, 2ch, 8htr, (2htr in next st) twice, 8htr, (2htr in next st) twice, 16htr, (2htr in next st) twice, 8htr, (2htr in next st) twice, 8htr (64 sts).

Row 4: Turn, 2ch, 9htr, (2htr in next st) twice, 10htr, (2htr in next st) twice, 18htr, (2htr in next st) twice, 10htr, (2htr in next st) twice, 9htr (72 sts).

Rows 5–12: Cont to work rows back and forth, increasing as in previous rows by working an extra st before first set of 2 increases and after the fourth set, and 2 extra sts between first and second, second and third, and third and fourth sets of increases. The 2 increases should be worked in centre 2 of 4htr of previous row.

Row 12 will be: turn, 2ch, 17htr, (2htr in next st) twice, 26htr, (2htr in next st) twice, 34htr, (2htr in next st) twice, 26htr, (2htr in next st) twice, 17htr (136 sts).

Round 13: DO NOT TURN. From now on, sweater will be crocheted in rounds and in this round you'll exclude the sleeves. Start with a sl st in first htr of the previous row (to close round), 1ch, 20dc, miss 28 sts of sleeve, 40dc, miss 28 sts of sleeve, 20dc (80dc). Close with sl st in first dc.

Rounds 14–20: Cont in round with 2ch, 80tr. Close with sl st in first tr. After round 20, fasten off.

Round 21: Using coral pink, 2ch, 80tr in back loop of sts. Using dark blue, close with sl st in first tr. Fasten off coral pink.

Round 22: Using dark blue, 2ch, 80tr in back loop of sts. Using coral pink, close with sl st in first tr. Fasten off dark blue.

Round 23: Using coral pink, 2ch, 80tr in back loop of sts. Using dark blue, close with sl st in first tr. Fasten off coral pink.

Round 24: Using dark blue, 2ch, 80tr in back loop of sts. Close with sl st in first tr.

Round 25: 2ch, 80tr. Close with sl st in first tr.

Round 26: 1ch, work 80 reverse dc. Fasten off and weave in ends.

Finishing

Using coral pink, crochet a round of reverse dc around both armholes.

Using dark blue, crochet a round of dc around neck opening, working approximately 3dc for every 2 rows and making 3 button loops on 1 edge by working 2ch, missing 1 row end. Attach buttons securely (see page 92).

Yarn:
4 ply weight
55% wool/33% acrylic/
12% cashmere
(125 m/137 yd, 50 g/1¾ oz)
- 2 balls light blue
- 1 ball teal

Hook: 3.5 mm (US E-4)

Notions: 3 buttons, approx. 1.5 cm (⅝ in) wide

Tension: 18 sts x 10 rows = 10 cm (4 in) square over tr

Size: 44.5 cm (17½ in) chest, 20.5 cm (8 in) length, 11.5 cm (4½ in) underarm sleeve length
Fits 0- to 3-month-old baby

Special stitches: dc foundation chain (see page 109)
Reverse dc (see page 110)
Back loop (see page 118)

To make the long sleeved sweater

Using light blue and teal, crochet short-sleeved sweater according to pattern on page 89.

Adding the sleeves

Row 1: Using light blue, join yarn with sl st in third st from armpit at back of sleeve. 2ch, 31tr around armhole. Close with sl st in first tr.

Rows 2–7: 2ch, tr2tog in back loop, 1tr in every back loop all around. Close with sl st in tr2tog, using teal in row 7. This results in tr2tog + 24tr in row 7. Fasten off light blue yarn.

Row 8: Using teal, 2ch, tr2tog in back loop, 23tr in back loop. Using light blue, close with sl st in tr2tog. Fasten off teal yarn.

Row 9: Using light blue, 2ch, tr2tog in back loop, 22tr in back loop. Using teal, close with sl st in tr2tog. Fasten off light blue yarn.

Row 10: Using teal, 2ch, tr2tog in back loop, 21tr in back loop. Using light blue, close with sl st in tr2tog. Fasten off teal yarn.

Row 11: Using light blue, 2ch, tr2tog in back loop, 20tr in back loop. Close with sl st in tr2tog.

Row 12: 2ch, 21tr. Close with sl st in first tr.

Row 13: 1ch, work 21 reverse dc. Fasten off and weave in ends.

Work both sleeves in same way.

Attaching buttons

Push yarn needle and yarn through crochet and then through 1 hole in button, then loop back through another hole in button and take needle back through crochet. Repeat this until button is firmly attached.

Now push needle back through crochet so that yarn is behind button.

Wrap yarn around anchoring yarn several times until button is secure.

Push needle back through to WS of crochet and fasten off.

Sleepy sheep mobile

Make this cute mobile for endless sheep counting and restful sleep for your little one. Natural yarns give the sheep a lovely, realistic look.

Yarn:
2 ply weight
95% wool/5% cashmere
(380 m/416 yd, 100 g/3½ oz)
• 1 ball each cream; brown; taupe

Hook: 3.25 mm (US D-3)

Notions: Wooden mobile approx. 28 cm x 28 cm (11 in x 11 in), wadding for stuffing

Tension: 6 bobbles x 16 rows = 10 cm (4 in) over bobble patt

Size: Dependent on wooden mobile used

Special stitches: dc foundation chain (see page 109)
Bobble of 4htr (see page 111)
Popcorn of 3tr (see page 113)

To make the mobile

For each sheep, choose a main colour and second colour. The main colour is used for body and second colour for tail and legs.

Using main colour, work 3ch. Close into a circle with sl st.

Round 1: 1ch, 6dc in circle. Close with sl st in first dc.

Round 2: 1ch, 2dc in every st. Close with sl st in first dc (12 sts).

Round 3: 1ch, *2dc, 2dc in next st, rep from * 3 times. Close with sl st in first dc (16 sts).

Round 4: 1ch, 5dc. In next st to make first ear: sl st, 2ch, popcorn of 3tr, 2ch, sl st in same st. 4dc, make a matching second ear. 5dc, close with sl st in first dc. Fasten off.

Using scraps

This is enough yarn for a flock of sheep. If you have leftover bits of yarn from other projects, that could work just as well.

Round 5: Attach second colour with sl st in st where you stopped after round 4, 1ch, 1dc in every st, going behind ears so they pop up at front (16dc). Close with sl st in first dc.

Round 6: 1ch, 16dc, don't close.

Round 7: *1ch, bobble of 4htr in next dc, 1ch, 1dc, rep from * 6 times. 1ch, 1 more bobble, 1ch, miss last dc, instead make dc in top of first bobble. This is first round of 8 bobbles.

Safety first!

This is a decorative piece only. Hang it well out of baby's reach and not directly above a cot or crib.

Rounds 8–15: Now work in continuous rounds in spiral style by not closing with a sl st at end of each round. *1ch, bobble of 4htr in next dc, 1ch, 1dc in top of next bobble. Rep from * to work 7 rounds of 8 bobbles.

Decrease round 1: *1dc in next bobble, miss dc, 1dc in next bobble. 1ch, bobble in next dc, 1ch, rep from * 3 times (4 bobbles).

Stuff sheep lightly, making sure you get some stuffing in back of sheep's face.

Decrease round 2: Make last 4 bobbles by going into 2dc of previous round. *1ch, work 2htr bobble loops in first dc, work 2htr bobble loops in second dc. Finish bobble normally, rep from * 3 times. Fasten off and sew closed.

Tail

Using second colour, work a dc foundation ch of 3 sts. Weave in 1 end and use other end to attach tail to sheep.

Legs

Using second colour, work 3ch and close into a circle with sl st. 1ch, 6dc in circle. Don't close; cont making another 12dc. St leg to body. Rep 3 times. For variation, you could attach legs a little off-centre from face; it looks very cute.

Assembly

Using string, attach sheep to mobile, with 2 above/below each other on middle hook and 1 sheep at each end. You could add a little bedtime music box to the mobile if you like.

Use stitch markers

If you find it hard to keep track of your rounds when working in spirals, use a st marker in the first bobble of every round.

Chapter Four

CROCHET TECHNIQUES

The projects in this book use basic crochet stitches, plus some structure stitches and some increase and decrease stitching. All are explained here, along with the traditional granny square.

Please feel free to play around with textured stitches to create your own unique pieces. They are so much fun! Textured stitches are my personal favourites, and babies love exploring the varied surfaces they create.

Getting started

Holding the hook and yarn

There are two ways to hold the hook: the knife hold and the pencil hold. Use the one you find most comfortable. To create tension on the yarn so that you can form stitches evenly, hold the working yarn in your non-dominant hand.

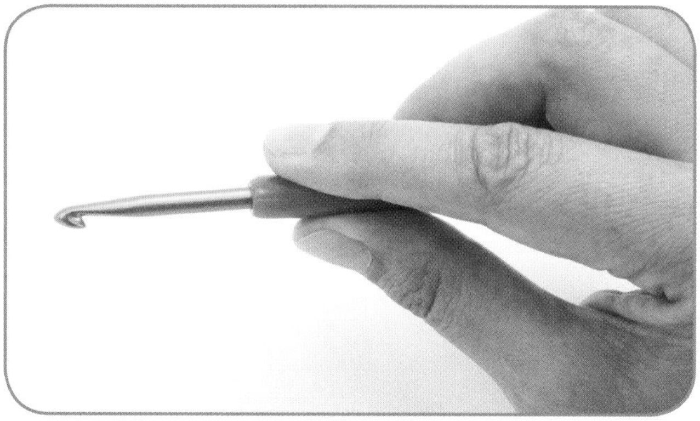

Knife hold

Hold the flat section or middle of the hook lightly between your thumb and forefinger.

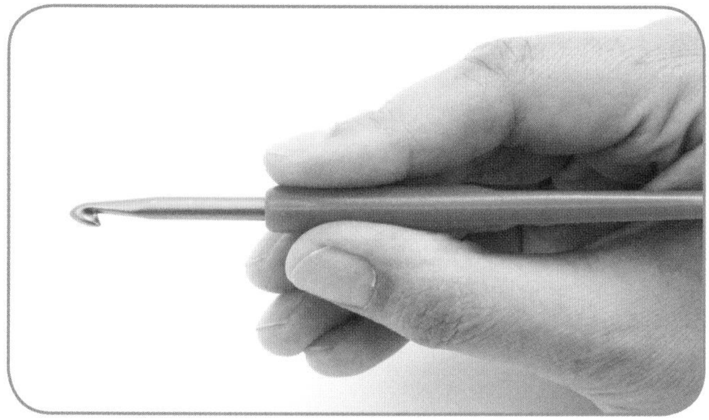

Pencil hold

Use the tips of your thumb and forefinger to hold the hook lightly on the flat section or middle of the hook.

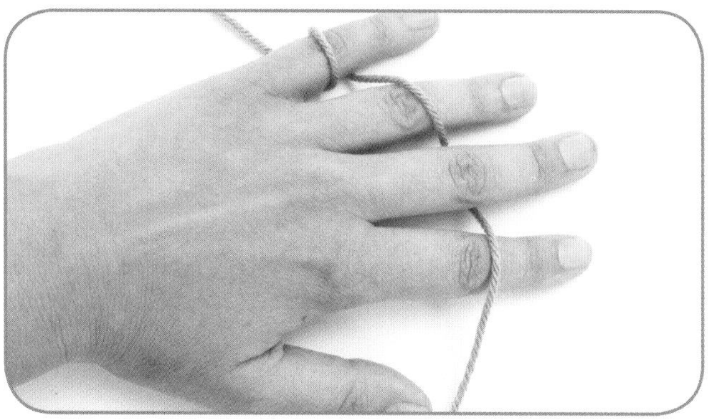

Woven

Weave the yarn over your index finger, under the middle finger, and over your ring finger. If this feels loose, wrap it around your little finger.

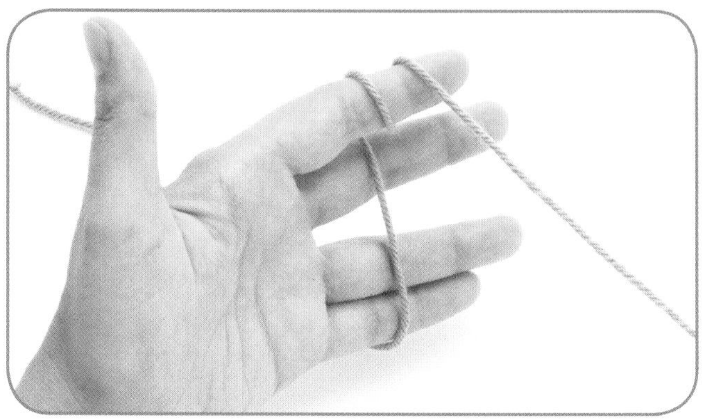

Forefinger

Wrap the yarn twice around your forefinger.

Making a slipknot

Wrap the yarn clockwise around your forefinger and cross it over the working yarn, leaving a 15 cm (6 in) tail (you will weave this in later). Insert the hook in front of the original loop but behind the tail end of the yarn. Slide the loop off your finger while pinching the X overlap you just made. Hold both yarn ends and pull them tight, but not too tight, around your hook.

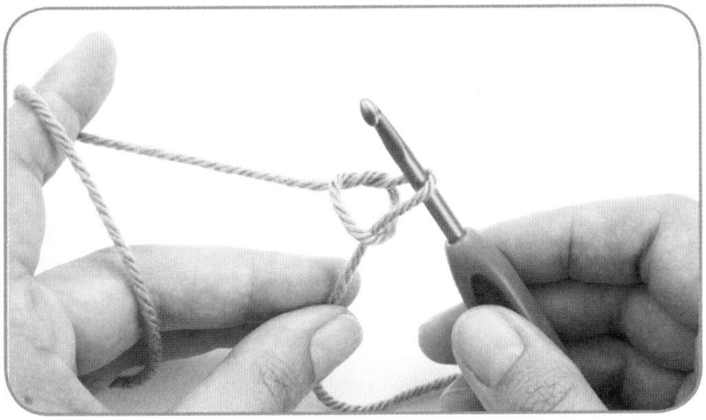

Using stitch markers

Stitch markers are a useful tool to help you keep track of your crochet. Use them to mark the position of the end of a round; to count multiples of stitches; to remind you which is the front or back of your work; or where the pattern indicates a change in stitches. It's best to use removable stitch markers.

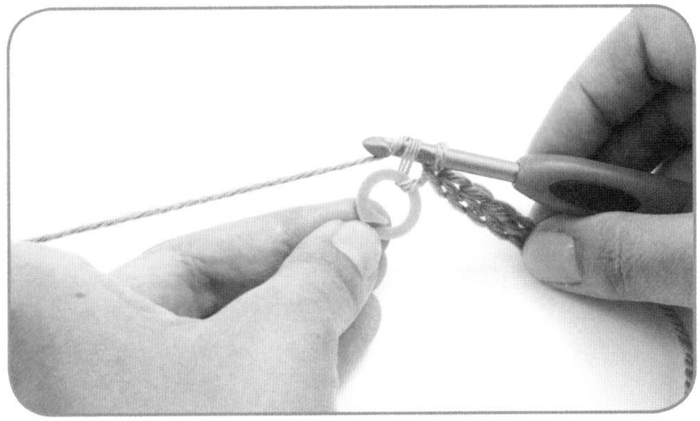

Tension

For many projects in this book, checking and maintaining your tension to ensure that your finished crochet is the correct size is not essential. However, it is necessary for some items and, for these, you should work a swatch before you start.

Each pattern will indicate the tension. For example: 15 sts x 9 rows = 10 cm (4 in) square over treble crochet (tr) using 5 mm (US H-8) hook. However, everyone's tension is different.

To check your tension, crochet a 15¼ cm (6 in) square using the yarn, hook size, and stitch pattern (in this example, treble crochet) stated in the pattern. Place a ruler horizontally across a row of stitches in the centre of the square and insert pins at the 0 and 25 cm (4 in) marks. Then count the stitches between the pins – including any partial stitches. For this example, do you have 15 stitches? If you have too many, make a second square using a hook one size larger. If you have too few, use a hook one size smaller. Keep making squares until you have the correct tension. Check the vertical tension in the same way, counting the number of rows between the pins – including any partial rows – and adjust the hook size as necessary.

Basic stitches

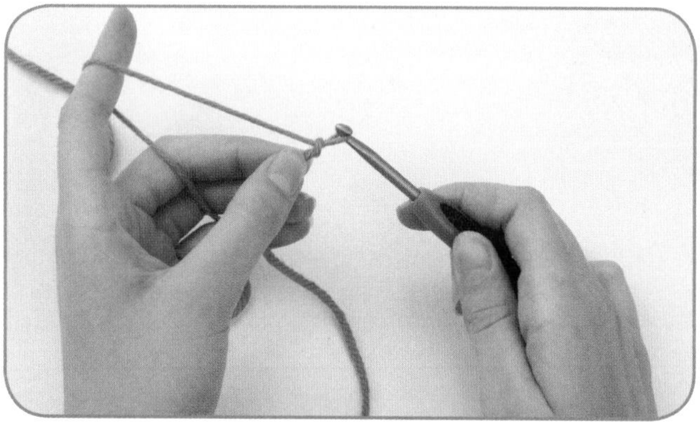

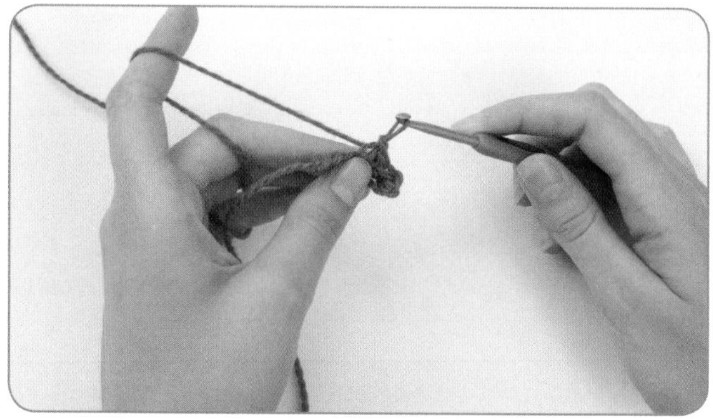

Foundation chain and chain stitch (ch)

The foundation chain is a little like casting on when knitting—it's the starting point for working new stitches. Make a slipknot on your hook and hold it with the thumb and middle finger of your yarn hand. Bring the working yarn from behind and around the hook (this is referred to as a 'yarn around the hook'). Use the hook to pull the yarn through the loop on your hook. You have made one chain stitch. Repeat to make the required number of chains, but remember that the loop on your hook never counts as a chain stitch. As you work the chain, keep moving your fingers up the chain to hold the latest stitch.

Slip stitch (sl st)

Slip stitch is rarely used to create crochet fabrics on its own. Instead it is used to join crochet fabrics, work across a set of stitches without adding height, join rounds, or reinforce an edge.

To create a slip stitch in a foundation chain, insert the hook into the second chain from the hook. Yarn around the hook and draw it through the loop on the hook. The slip stitch can also be used to add a decorative row around your crochet work (see page 115).

Turning chains

Turning chains are essential to bring the first stitch of a row or round up to the proper height. This is why a pattern will tell you to miss chains before you work your first stitch into the foundation chain. A slip stitch does not require a turning chain. Single crochet has one chain but this is not counted as a stitch. Half treble crochet has two turning chains; these sometimes count as a stitch. Treble crochet requires three turning chains and these are counted as a stitch. Four chains are used with double treble crochet and these also count as a stitch.

Double crochet (dc)

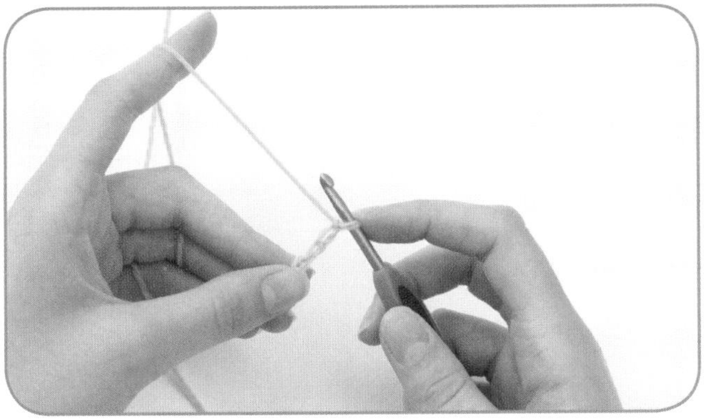

1 Insert the hook into the second chain from the hook.

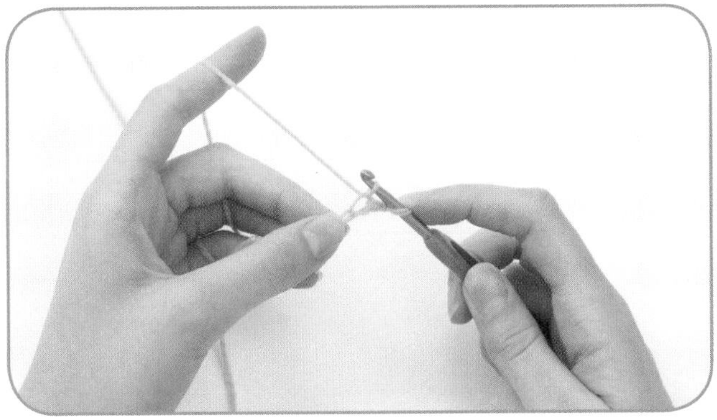

2 Yarn around the hook and pull up a loop to make two loops on the hook.

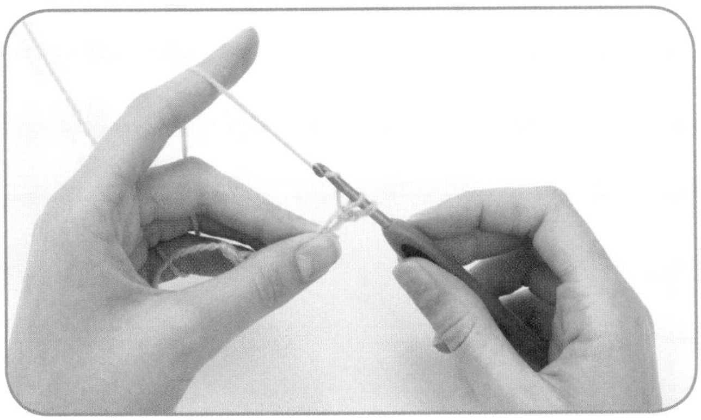

3 Yarn around the hook and pull it through both loops on the hook to complete the stitch. Insert the hook into the next chain and repeat steps 2 and 3. Repeat this sequence in each chain.

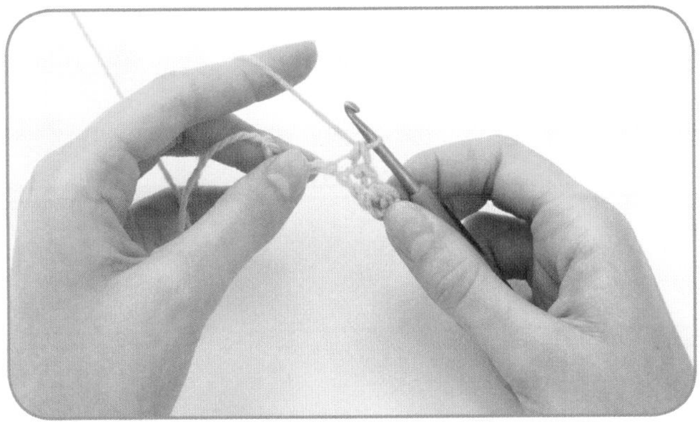

4 To work the next row, make one chain and turn the work. Insert the hook into the first stitch under the top two loops and complete steps 2 and 3. Continue across the row. Do not work a stitch into the turning chain of the previous row.

Half treble crochet (htr)

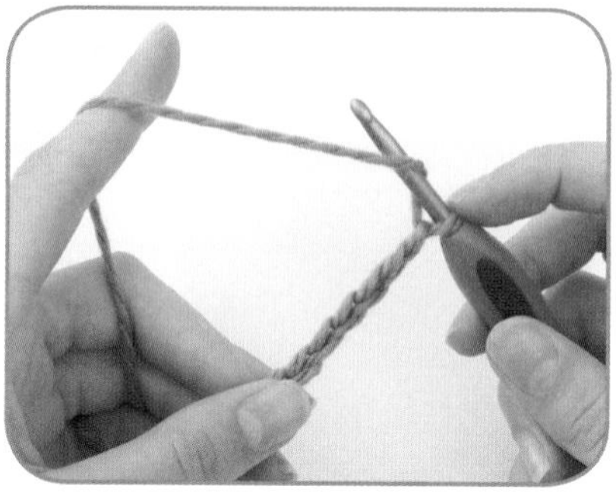

1 Yarn around the hook and insert the hook into the third chain from the hook.

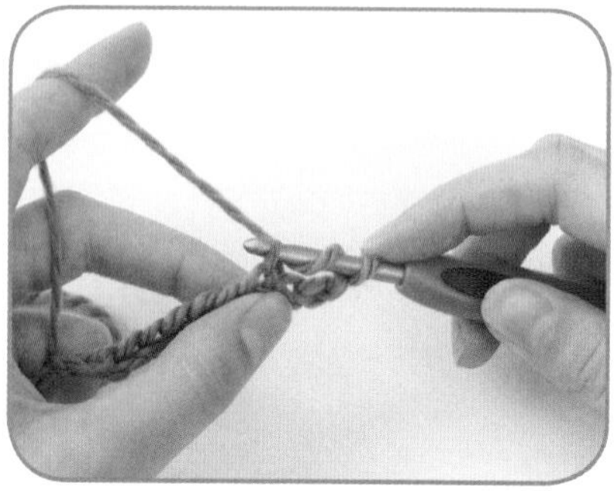

2 Yarn around the hook and pull up a loop to make three loops on the hook.

3 Yarn around the hook and draw through all three loops on the hook to complete the stitch. Yarn around the hook, insert the hook into the next chain, and complete steps 2 and 3. Repeat in each chain across.

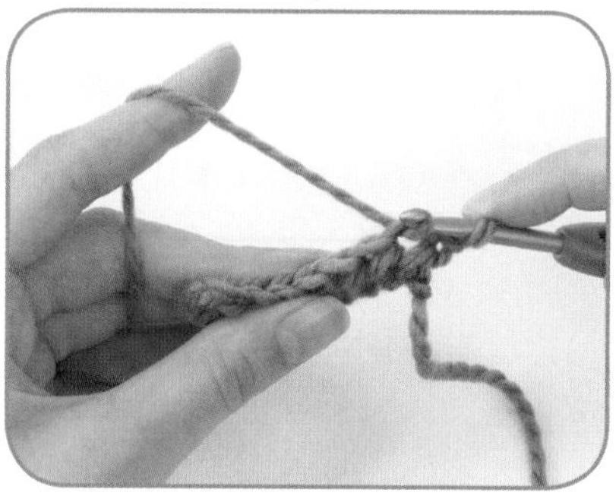

4 To work the next row, make two chains and turn the work. Insert the hook into the second stitch (missing the first stitch because the two turning chains count as a stitch).

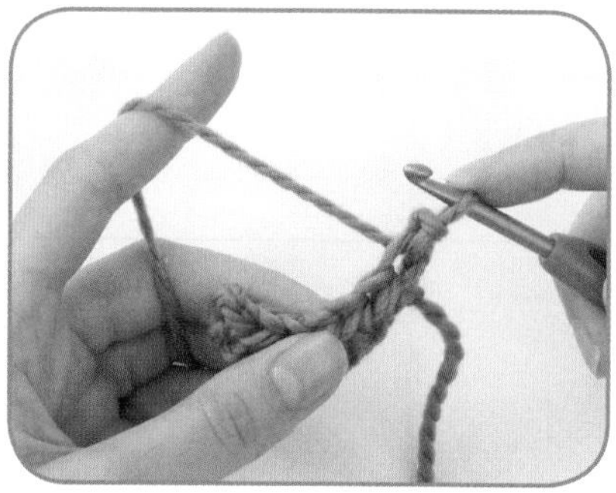

5 Work under the top two loops and complete steps 2 and 3. Continue working stitches into each stitch across the row. Make the last stitch into the top chain of the previous row's turning chain.

Counting the two turning chains as a stitch can leave gaps in the row edges. As a result, some patterns do not count them as a stitch. If this is the case, work the first stitch of the row into the first stitch, and do not work a stitch into the turning chain at the end of the row. Follow the pattern instructions closely and make sure the stitch count for each row or round matches the stitch count given in the pattern.

Treble crochet (tr)

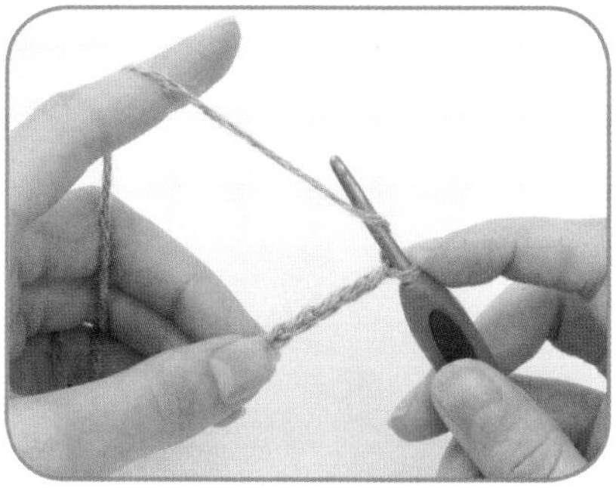

1 Yarn around the hook and insert the hook into the fourth chain from the hook.

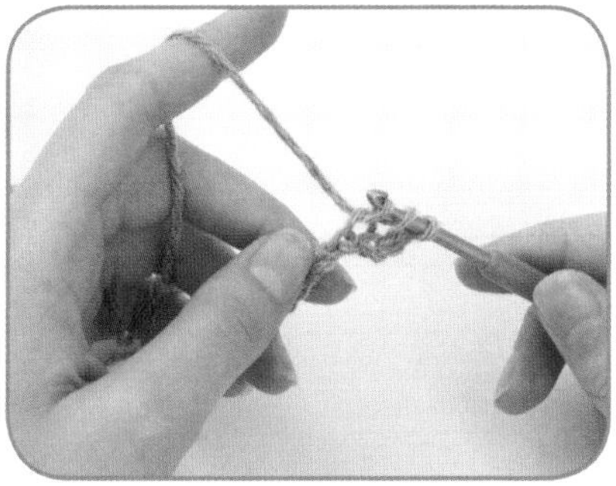

2 Yarn around the hook and pull up a loop to make three loops on the hook.

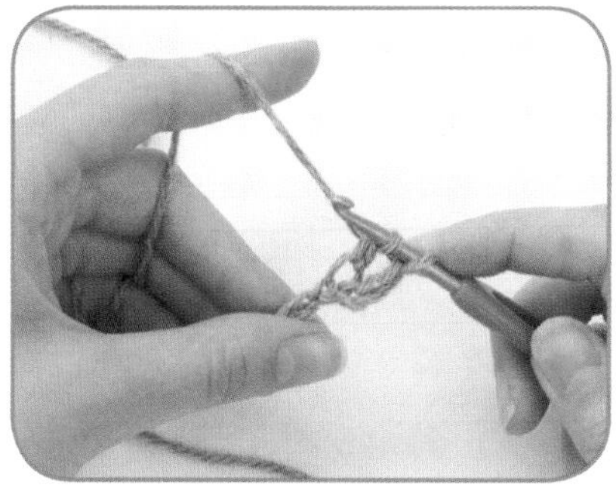

3 Yarn around the hook and draw through two loops. There will be two loops on the hook.

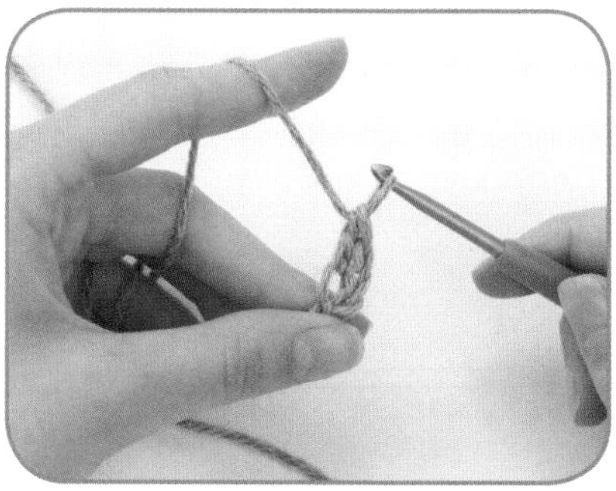

4 Yarn around the hook and draw through two loops to complete the stitch. Yarn around the hook, insert the hook into the next chain, and complete steps 2 to 4. Repeat in each chain across.

5 To work the next row, make three chains and turn the work. Insert the hook into the second stitch (missing the first stitch because the three turning chains count as a stitch). Work under the top two loops and complete steps 2 to 4.

6 Continue working stitches into each stitch across the row. The last stitch will be made into the top chain of the previous row's turning chain.

Double treble crochet (dtr)

1 Yarn around the hook twice and insert the hook into the fifth chain from the hook.

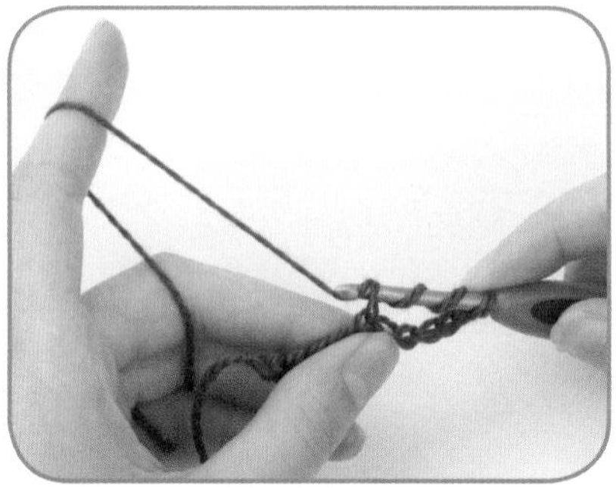

2 Yarn around the hook and pull up a loop to make four loops on the hook.

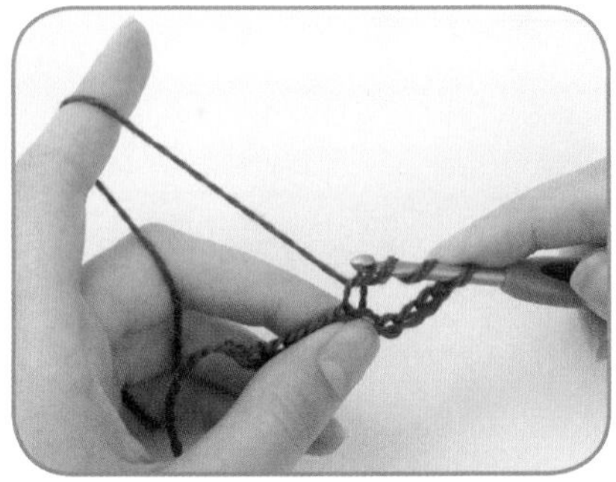

3 Yarn around the hook and draw through two loops. There will be three loops on the hook.

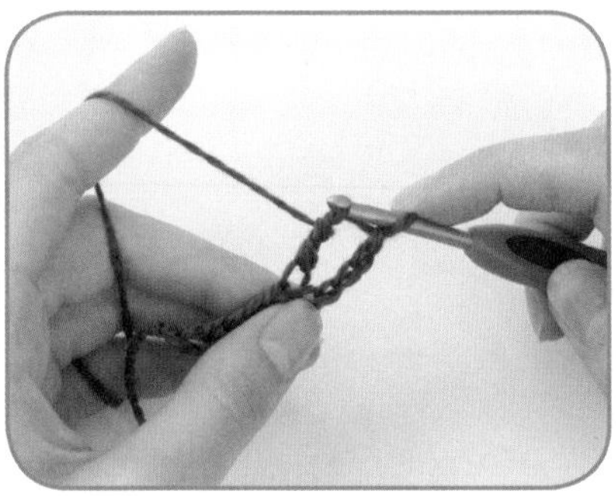

4 Yarn around the hook and draw through two loops. There will be two loops on the hook.

5 Yarn around the hook and draw through two loops to complete the stitch. Yarn around the hook twice, insert the hook into the next chain, and complete steps 2 to 5. Repeat in each chain across.

6 To work the next row, make four chains and turn the work. Insert the hook into the second stitch (missing the first stitch because the four turning chains count as a stitch). Work under the top two loops and complete steps 2 to 5. Continue across the row. Make the last stitch into the top chain of the previous row's turning chain.

Increasing and decreasing stitches

Double crochet decrease (dc2tog)

1 Insert the hook into the first stitch and pull up a loop. Insert the hook into the next stitch and pull up a loop. There will be three loops on the hook.

2 Yarn around the hook and draw through all three loops to complete the decrease.

Half treble crochet decrease (htr2tog)

1 Yarn around the hook, insert the hook into the first stitch, and pull up a loop. Yarn around the hook, insert the hook into the next stitch, and pull up a loop. There will be five loops on the hook. For a less bulky half treble crochet decrease, omit this yarn around the hook.

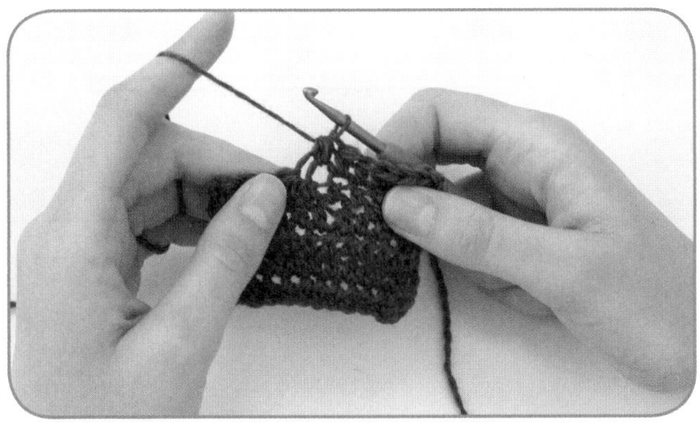

2 Yarn around the hook and draw through all five loops to complete the decrease.

Treble crochet decrease (tr2tog)

1 Yarn around the hook, insert the hook into the first stitch, and pull up a loop. Yarn around the hook and draw through two loops on the hook. Yarn around the hook, insert the hook into the next stitch, and pull up a loop. Yarn around the hook and draw through two loops. There will be three loops on the hook.

2 Yarn around the hook and draw through all three loops to complete the decrease.

Increase within a row

Work more than one stitch into a stitch of the previous row or round. Here the increase is shown in treble crochet, but the method is the same for all the other crochet stitches.

Increase at end of row

1 Work extended stitches. For extended double crochet, insert the hook into the same stitch as the last treble crochet of the row. *Pull up a loop, yarn around the hook, and draw through one loop only. Mark the chain stitch you have just made.

2 Yarn around the hook and draw through the two loops on your hook to complete the stitch. Insert your hook into the marked chain and repeat from * to create the next stitch.

Increase at beginning of row

Work the number of turning chains required for the stitch plus an extra chain for each additional stitch you want to add. Miss the required number of turning chains and then work a stitch into the remaining chains to complete the increase.

Special stitches

Double crochet foundation chain (dc foundation chain)

This is used to create a more flexible edge, mostly for garments in this book.

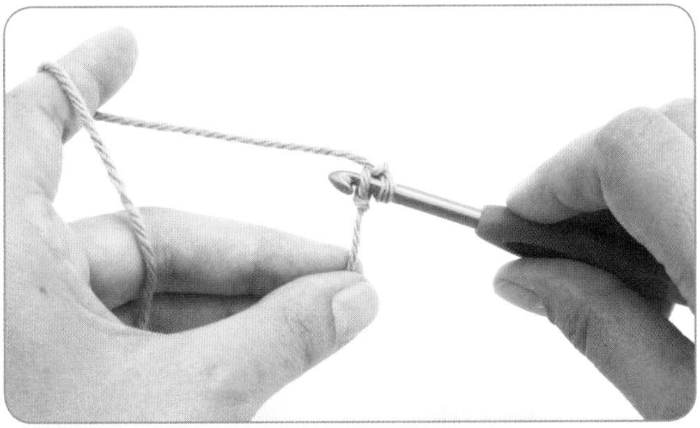

1 Chain 2 and then make a double crochet in the first chain.

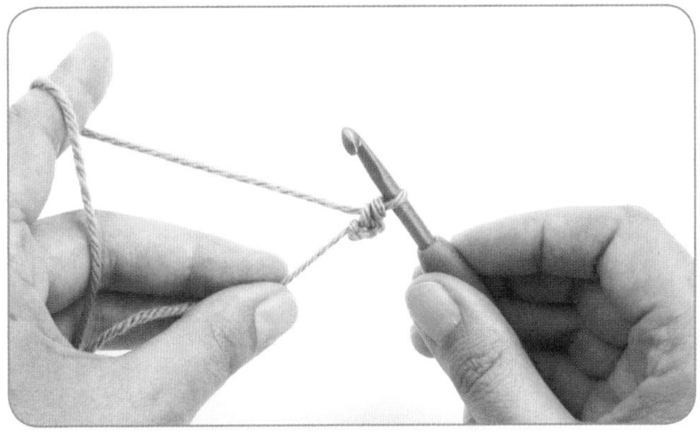

2 Looking at the stitch from the side, insert the hook in the double crochet you have just made.

3 Make another double crochet.

4 Continue making a double crochet stitch into side of the previous one.

Reverse double crochet (reverse dc)

Use reverse double crochet for decorative edgings. It's worked like a regular double crochet, but you work into the stitch behind your hook instead of the one in front of it. You are literally going into the work in reverse of your crochet, creating double crochet stitches that bend over to the back of the work.

1 Insert the hook, from back to front, in the next stitch to the right.

2 Yarn around the hook.

3 Draw the yarn through the stitch.

4 Yarn around the hook and draw it through the two loops on the hook.

Bobble stitches

There are bobbles in this book made of htr stitches and tr stitches, as well as popcorns.

Bobble made of htr stitches

1 Yarn around, insert hook into stitch, and pull yarn back through stitch.

2 Instead of finishing this stitch with a yarn around and pulling through all three loops on the hook, you are going to leave the loops on the hook and start a new htr with yarn around.

3 Insert hook into the same stitch and pull yarn back through stitch.

4 Depending on the pattern, you are going to start a new htr 3, 4, or 5 times and THEN yarn around and pull through all loops at once.

The nice thing about this stitch is that it appears the same at the front and back of your work, making it perfect for blankets and other items that need to look the same on both sides.

Bobble made of tr stitches

1 Yarn around, insert hook into stitch, and pull yarn back through stitch. Yarn around and pull through two loops on hook.

2 Leave the loops on the hook and start a new tr in the same stitch with yarn around insert hook into stitch, yarn around and pull yarn back through stitch, yarn around and pull through two loops. Continue like this 2 or 3 times, depending on the pattern.

3 Yarn around and pull through all loops on hook.

The bobble pops out at the back of your work, so is most often worked in the wrong side to make it visible at the front. Usually this stitch is worked in a row of dc to make the large stitch bobble pop up even more.

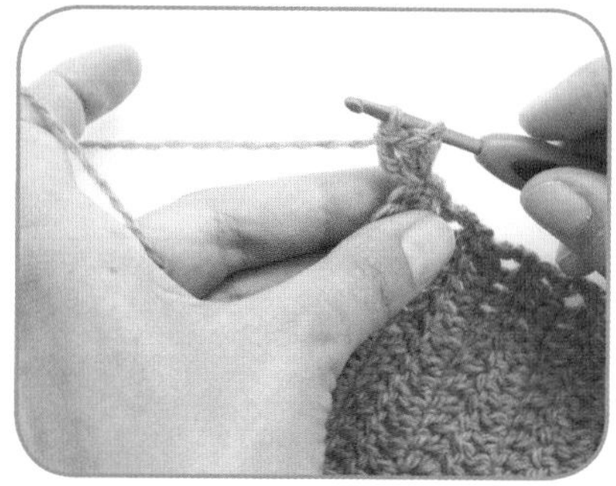

Popcorn made of 3tr stitches

1 2ch, make 3tr in the next stitch. Pull up a loop and take the hook out of your work.

2 Insert the hook from back to front into the second beginning chain and then straight into the loop you just pulled up.

3 Tighten the yarn to your hook and then yarn around hook.

4 Pull it through the loop and second beginning chain.

Pulling through the loop and beg ch tightens the 3tr at the top and makes it pop at the back of the work. Of course, you can make even larger popcorns by adding 1 or 2 tr. By going in with your hook from front to back, you'll create a popcorn that pops at the front of your work.

Stripes

1 Work your way to the final stitch of your first colour and use the hook to pull up a loop.

2 Yarn around with the second colour and pull through the stitch. This joins the new colour yarn to the work You can now continue to work the pattern, adding a stripe of colour into the design.

Granny square pattern

1 3ch and close into a circle with a sl st in the first ch.
Round 1: 4ch (counts as 1tr and 2ch), * 3tr into circle, 2ch, rep from * twice, 2tr into circle, close with sl st into 3ch at beg of round. (Square of 4 x clusters of 3tr, divided by 2ch corners.)

2 Round 2: sl st into next 2chcorner, ch3 (counts as 1tr and 2ch), 3tr into same corner, * work (3tr, 2ch, 3tr) into next corner, rep from * twice, then work 2tr into corner where you started, sl st into 3ch at beg of round. (Square of 4 x 2clusters of 3tr, divided by 2ch corners.)

3 On next and every following round work 3tr, 2ch 3tr into each corner and 3tr into each 2chsp along straight sides. Close round with sl st into 3ch at beg of rounds.

Decorative stitch

Using a little leftover yarn, you can add a decorative row on or around your crochet work using a slip stitch.

1 With the yarn at the back, insert the hook from front to back into your work.

2 Yarn around the hook and pull up a loop through your work.

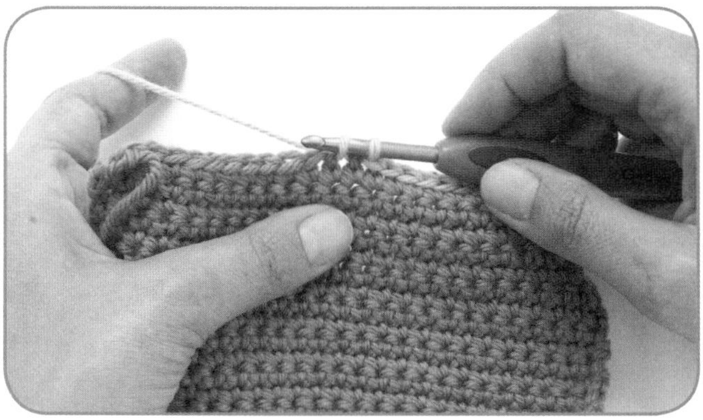

3 Pull the loop through the loop on your hook.

4 Insert hook into next stitch and repeat steps 2 and 3 across the row. Make sure to draw up a loop that's long enough to lay easily on your work, and don't pull it too tight. It looks like embroidery!

Spike stitch

1 Insert the hook from front to back through the designated stitch two or more rows below. The number of rows down will determine how long the spike stitch is.

2 Yarn around the hook.

3 Draw the yarn through the stitch and pull the loop back up to the working level.

4 Yarn around the hook and draw the yarn through the two loops on your hook.

5 Continue to work until you are ready to add another spike stitch.

Spike stitch fabric

Keep in mind that spike stitch results in a very stiff fabric without much flexibility, so it's best used for projects with a more structured look.

Front post treble crochet (fptr)

1 Yarn around the hook and insert the hook from the front to the back of the fabric, taking it around the back of the post of the stitch, and bring it out at the front of the fabric. Yarn around the hook again and pull up a loop on the right side of the fabric (three loops on hook).

2 Yarn around the hook and draw it through the first two loops on the hook. Yarn around the hook again and draw it through the remaining two loops (one front post double crochet made).

Back post treble crochet (bptr)

1 Yarn around the hook and insert the hook from the back to the front, taking it around the front of the post of the stitch, and bring it out at the back of the crochet. Yarn around the hook again and pull up a loop on the wrong side of the fabric (three loops on hook).

2 Yarn around the hook and draw it through the first two loops on the hook.

3 Yarn around the hook again and draw it through the remaining two loops (one back post double crochet made).

Front and back loop stitches

Front and back loop stitches are often used when two crochet pieces are joined together and you don't want a bulky join.

Front loop stitches

If you look at the top of your stitches, you'll see that each double crochet, half treble crochet, treble crochet and double treble crochet forms a 'V' shape. Front loop only stitches are made by inserting your hook into just the front loop, not through both loops. The front loop will always be the one closest to you when you are holding your crochet. Once you have inserted the hook into the front loop, you can then follow the pattern to make the next stitch as usual.

Back loop stitches

Back loop only stitches are made by inserting your hook into the back loop only, not through both loops. The back loop will always be the one farthest away from you when you are holding your crochet. Once you have inserted the hook into the back loop, you can then follow the pattern to make the next stitch as usual.

Seams and joining

Joining new colours

Whether you need to join in a new colour of yarn at the beginning or in the middle of a row, the method is the same. Use the same technique for joining in a new ball of the same yarn colour, but note that joining is best done at the beginning of a row.

1 Work the last stitch but stop at the last step before drawing through the final yarn around the hook. There will be two loops on the hook.

2 Drop the old colour behind the work and draw the new colour through to complete the stitch. Continue working with the new colour as usual.

Joining sections

Take time when sewing your crochet sections together so that the finished item is neat and reflects the time you have taken to create it. There are several ways to join seams, and you can use more than one method in a project if you wish. If you want a hidden seam, then mattress stitch is a good choice. Use the same yarn you used to crochet the item. If you want the seam to become part of the finished design, choose a slip stitch or a single crochet seam. You could also use a contrasting yarn color to add decorative detail.

Mattress stitch

This seam has no bulk and is used frequently in garment construction. Place the crocheted pieces on a flat surface with the right sides facing up, making sure the stitches are aligned. Insert the yarn needle through the post of the bottom-right stitch, cross over to the corresponding left stitch, and at the same time draw the yarn through the post of the stitch. Continue working backward and forward through the posts of the stitches. Gently tighten the seam while you work, but don't make it too tight.

Top seams

Top seams can be joined with double crochet (see page 103) or slip stitch (see page 102). Slip stitch creates a flat seam but it will not have as much stretch as a double crochet seam.

Slip stitch seam

Hold the two pieces of crochet to be joined with right sides facing each other. Insert the hook through the first stitch of both pieces, and pull the yarn through to make a slip stitch. Insert the hook through the next stitch of both pieces, yarn around the hook, and pull the yarn through both the stitches and the loop on the hook. Continue to the end of the seam.

Double crochet seam

Work in the same way as slip stitch, using double crochet.

Whip stitch

This stitch is quick to work and is especially useful on straight-edged fabrics. It's a good choice for joining motifs together. With the right sides of the fabric pieces held together, insert the yarn needle from the front to the back of a stitch and through the corresponding stitch on the other piece. Bring the needle to the front again and repeat until the seam is finished.

Back stitch

This sturdy seam has some bulk to it, so test it first to see if it's an appropriate seam for your crochet fabric. With the right sides of the fabric pieces held together and working about one stitch space away from the edge of the fabric, insert the yarn needle from the back to the front through both layers. Insert the needle from the front to the back of the fabric and then bring it up through to the front again, one stitch beyond the working yarn. For the next stitch, insert the needle from the front to the back in the same place as the last stitch ended and again bring the needle to the front, one stitch beyond the working yarn. Repeat until the seam is finished.

Joining granny squares as you go

1 After every cluster of 3tr, add a sl st in the space between the opposite 3tr clusters on the previous square.

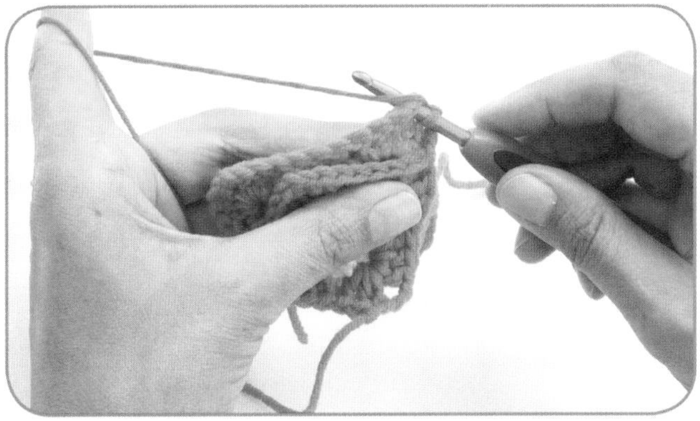

2 In the corners, make a sl st and 1ch.

3 Continue following the granny square pattern. After making each cluster of 3tr along the side, work a sl st in the gap between the opposite clusters of 3tr on the side of the previous square.

4 Continue joining squares in this manner.

Finishing

Fastening off

To fasten off your project, you will need make sure that the yarn end is pulled tightly so that your project will not unravel.

1 Pull up a little loop in the last stitch with your hook, cut the yarn leaving a tail of 10 cm to 15¼ cm (4 in to 6 in) and with your hook, pull on that loop until the yarn end goes through.

2 Pull tightly and you are ready to weave in the ends.

Weaving in ends

Using a yarn needle, go through your stitches on the wrong side of the work for about 10 stitches. Move up or down a row, and go through the back of the stitches in the other direction. Fasten off the yarn. I prefer not to tie knots; however, there are some exceptions: when using highly slippery yarn (not used in this book), or with baby items, such as toys, where the baby will be pulling and stretching the yarn. In these cases, I recommend tying a knot first and then weaving in the ends.

Blocking

In a room without much direct sunlight or warmth, prepare a blocking mat, or cover a spare bed with towels. Soak the item in cool or lukewarm water. For the floor blanket, don't soak it, but wet it gently. Carefully lay the item out on the mat and pin it into the desired shape. Let dry. It may take the blanket a day or two due to the chunky yarn.

Cross-stitch embroidery

Double crochet stitches are quite tight and can be used as an embroidery mesh. Use the stitches as a 'fabric' to work your cross-stitch on using a yarn needle. With the right side of your work facing you, approach the fabric with the needle from the back and come out at the front (bottom right of the X). Take the needle back in at the top left of the stitch (top left of the the X). Bring the needle out in the top-right corner and go in at the bottom left. You should now have one embroidered cross-stitch; repeat to form your chosen design.

Reading patterns

Crochet patterns are like handwriting: very personal and written according to the logic of the writer. This means patterns from some designers may be easier for you to read than others, but designers have their own style and once you have followed more patterns, you'll begin to understand their signature. In this book I have used abbreviations for the stitches, combined with full sentences to guide you through the projects. Tips and tricks are given to provide you with ideas to personalize your projects.

Punctuation

Patterns are a concise and easy-to-read set of instructions that use abbreviations and punctuation to help avoid needless repetition.

Once you understand them, you will find that following the pattern becomes automatic.

( ) Parentheses give additional information about a pattern. For example, (12tr) listed at the end of a row says that you should have 12 treble crochet stitches when the row has been completed.

In this book, parentheses may also contain a stitch repeat—(1tr, 3ch, 1tr) twice. For this, you will work 1 treble crochet, 3chain, and 1 treble crochet all in the same stitch twice.

Ch 3 (counts as 1tr) explains that the three turning chains count as a treble crochet stitch and the stitch is included in the instructions for the stitch count at the end of the row or round.

*** Asterisks** indicate stitch instructions and pattern repeats on a row or round. For example, *Tr, 1ch, miss next st. Rep from * four times to last st, tr. This instruction tells you to work 1 treble crochet, 1 chain, miss next st. Repeat four more times, and then work 1treble crochet into the last stitch.

When there are two different pattern repeat instructions in the same row or round, the beginning of the second repeat is indicated with two asterisks, with the instruction to repeat from **.

You may also be asked to repeat a set of instructions between single and double asterisks: repeat from * to **.

Abbreviations

The patterns in this book feature a number of standard abbreviations, which are explained below:

( )	Work instructions within parentheses as many times as directed.
*****	Repeat instructions following or between specified asterisks as directed.
beg	begin(ning)
bptr	back post treble crochet
ch	chain or chain stitch
ch-	refers to chain or loop previously made, such as ch-2 loop
ch sp	chain space
cont	continue(ing)
dc	double crochet
dc2tog	double crochet 2 together
fptr	front post treble crochet
g	gram(s)
htr	half treble crochet
htr2tog	half treble crochet 2 together
m	meter(s)
mm	millimeter(s)
oz	ounce(s)
p	picot
patt	pattern
rep	repeat(s)
RS	right side
reverse dc	reverse double crochet
sl	slip
sl st	slip stitch
sp	space
st(s)	stitch(es)
tr	treble crochet
tr2tog	treble crochet 2 together
tog	together
WS	wrong side
yd	yard(s)

Index

Figures in **bold type** refer to photographs.

A, B, C

acrylic 45, 51, 77, 79, 82, 87, 89, 92
Autumnal colors mama scarf 20, **21**
blocking 122
bobbles 25, 45, 58, 60, 94, 111–113
Bright nursery bunting 25, **26, 27**
buttonholes 52, 85
cashmere 45, 51, 77, 79, 82, 87, 89, 92, 94
Chunky baby jacket 22, **23, 24**
Chunky floor blanket **36**, 37, **38**
Colourful bandana bibs **84**, 85
Complementary baby sweaters 89, **90, 91, 93**
cotton 25, 29, 30, 48, 54, 62, 71, 85
Cosy hot water bottle cover **42**, 43, **44**
cross stitch embroidery 122
Cute baby shorts **86**, 87, **88**

D, E, F

decorative rows 26, 57, 85, 102, 115
double crochet seam 120
Drawstring baby skirt 82, **83**
eco-friendly cotton 9
fastening off 122
finishing 122

G, H, J

gender neutral colours 9, 66
Granny square baby blanket 14, **15**
granny squares 14, 20, 30, 66, 114, 121
hook-and-loop tape 16, 52
hook and yarn, holding 100
joining 119–121

K, L, M

leftover yarn 94, 115
loops 103–108, 110–112, 116–118
merino 14, 17, 20, 22, 66
Motif nursery baskets 39, **40, 41**

N, O, P

Nautical coat hangers **70**, 71, **73**
Ombré baby sleeping bag **16**, 17, **18, 19**
Pastel waves nursery cushion 51, **52, 53**
Patchwork ball rattles **28**, 29
patterns, reading 123
popcorns 94, 111, 113

Q, R, S

quick projects 22, 85, 89
Rattle buddy 62, **63, 64**
Ribbon tie nappy case 30, **31, 32, 33**
seams 119–121
Sleepy sheep mobile 94, **95, 97**
Sleeveless cardigan 54, **55, 56, 57**
sleeves 24, 89, 92
slip stitch seam 120
slipknot, making 101
Snug mama shawl 45, **46, 47**
Snuggly cowl and hat 58, **59, 61**
Soft baby bonnet 66, **67, 68**
stitch markers, using 101
stitch
- back 120
- back post treble crochet 79, 117
- bobble 25, 45, 58, 60, 94, 111–113
- chain 102
- decorative 14, 20, 115
- double crochet 103, 109, 110,
- double crochet decrease 107
- double crochet foundation chain 102, 103, 109
- double treble crochet 51, 106
- foundation chain 58, 82, 92, 94, 102, 109
- front post treble crochet 117
- half treble crochet decrease 51–52, 85, 88, 107
- mattress 119
- reverse double crochet 82, 87, 92, 110
- slip 102
- spike 30, 116
- stripes 114
- treble crochet 105
- treble crochet decrease 108
- whip 120

stitches
- basic 102–106
- front and back loop 43, 77, 79, 82, 87, 118
- increasing and decreasing 107–108
- special 109–118

Striped baby beanie 79, **81**
Striped baby blanket 48, **49, 50**

T, U, V

toggle buttons 17, 22
top seams 120
toys 9, 29, 62
turning chains 102
Two tone baby booties 77, **76, 78**

W, Y, Z

waffle pattern 17–18
weaving in ends 122
whip stitch 120
yarn needles 92, 119, 120, 122
zigzag motif 41

Yarns Used in the Projects

Granny square baby blanket
Debbie Bliss Rialto DK; 100% Extra Fine Merino, 100 m/110 yd, 50 g/2 oz.
1 ball each in Gold 045, Tangerine 056, Cream 002; 2 balls each in Coral 055 and Deep rose 050; 4 balls in Mint.

Ombré baby sleeping bag
Debbie Bliss Rialto Chunky; 100% Extra Fine Merino, 60 m/65 yd, 50 g/2 oz.
5 balls in Cream 003;
4 balls each in Mint 038 and Teal 030; 2 balls in Green 037; 3 balls in Charcoal 022.

Autumnal mama scarf
Debbie Bliss Rialto DK; 100% extra fine Merino, 100 m/110 yd, 50 g/2 oz.
1 ball in Petunia 075; 2 balls each in Coral 055, Mint 054 and Deep rose 050. Scraps (left over from Granny Square Baby Blanket) in Gold 045, Tangerine 056 and Cream 002.

Chunky baby jacket
Debbie Bliss Rialto Chunky; 100% Extra Fine Merino, 60 m/65 yd, 50 g/2 oz.
5 balls in Cream 003.

Bright nursery bunting
Debbie Bliss Eco Baby; 100% Cotton, 125 m/136 yd, 50 g/2 oz.
1 ball each in Denim 29, Aqua 5, Mallard 39, Primrose 37, Blush 27, Rose 12 and Burnt Orange 33.

Patchwork ball rattles
Debbie Bliss Eco Baby; 100% Cotton, 125 m/136 yd, 50 g/2 oz.
For blue-green ball: 1 ball each in Sky 4, Primrose 37, White 1, Apple 6, Denim 29 and Aqua 5.
For multi-colored ball: 1 ball each in Blush 27, Apple 6, Rose 12, Sky 4, Primrose 37 and White 1.

Ribbon-tie nappy case
Debbie Bliss Cotton DK; 100% Cotton, 84 m/91 yd, 50 g/2 oz.
1 ball each in White 001, Light Blue 009, Beige 019 and Green 020;
3 balls in Navy 018.

Chunky floor blanket
Debbie Bliss Roma; 70% Wool, 30% Alpaca, 80 m/88 yd, 100 g/3½ oz.
6 balls in Steel 003; 5 balls in Ecru 001; 2 balls each in Rose 014 and Charcoal 018.

Motif nursery baskets
Debbie Bliss Roma; 70% Wool, 30% Alpaca, 80 m/88 yd, 100 g/3½ oz.
1 ball each in Rose 014 and Charcoal 018; scraps in Ecru 001 and Steel 003.

Cosy hot water bottle cover
Debbie Bliss Roma; 70% Wool 30% Alpaca, 80 m/88 yd, 100 g/ 3½ oz. 6 balls in Steel 003; 5 balls in Ecru 001; 2 balls each in Rose 014 and Charcoal 018.

Snug mama shawl
Debbie Bliss Cashmerino Aran; 55% Wool 33% Acrylic 12% Cashmere, 90 m/99 yd, 50 g/2 oz.
6 balls in Aqua 047; 2 balls in Mallard 056; 1 ball in Peach 072.

Striped baby blanket
Debbie Bliss Mia; 50% Wool 50% Cotton, 100 m/110 yd, 50 g/2 oz.
4 balls in Ecru 02; 2 balls each in Robin Egg 05, Corn 14 and Mallard 018; 1 ball in Sky 04.

Pastel waves nursery cushion
Debbie Bliss Cashmerino Aran; 55% Wool 33% Acrylic 12% Cashmere, 90 m/99 yd, 50 g/2 oz.
1 ball each in Duck Egg 82, Aqua 47, Indigo 57, Mulberry 42, Heather 46, Pale Lilac 71, Peach 72 and Coral 73.

Sleeveless cardigan
Debbie Bliss Mia; 50% Wool 50% Cotton, 110 yd/100 m, 50 g/2 oz.
2 balls in Ecru 02; 1 ball each in Robin Egg 05 and Mallard 18; scraps in Corn 14.

Snuggly cowl
Schachenmayr Baby Smiles Merino Wool; 100% Wool, 85 m/93 yd, 25 g/0.8 oz.
1 ball each in Red 30, Purple 49 and Peach 24.

Snuggly hat
Schachenmayr Baby Smiles Merino Wool; 100% Wool, 85 m/93 yd, 25 g/0.8 oz.
1 ball each in Red 30, Purple 49 and Peach 24.

Rattle buddy
Debbie Bliss Mia; 50% Wool 50% Cotton, 100 m/110 yd, 50 g/2 oz.
1 ball each in Ecru 02, Sky 04, Robin Egg 05 and Corn 14.

Soft baby bonnet
Debbie Bliss Rialto Lace; 100% Extra Fine Merino, 390 m/426 yd, 50 g/2 oz.
1 ball each in White 01 and Acid Yellow 035.

Nautical coat hangers
Debbie Bliss Eco Baby; 100% Cotton, 125 m/136 yd, 50 g/2 oz.
1 ball each in White 01, Red 22, Royal 35, Apple 06 and Baby Blue 40.

Two tone baby booties
Debbie Bliss Baby Cashmerino; 55% Wool, 33% Acrylic, 12% Cashmere, 125 m/136 yd, 50 g/2 oz.
1 ball each in 202 Light Blue and 203 Teal.

Striped baby beanie
Debbie Bliss Baby Cashmerino; 55% Wool, 33% Acrylic, 12% Cashmere, 125 m/136 yd, 50 g/2 oz.
1 ball each in Light Blue 202 and Teal 203.

Drawstring baby skirt
Debbie Bliss Baby Cashmerino; 55% Wool, 33% Acrylic, 12% Cashmere, 125 m/136 yd, 50 g/2 oz.
1 ball in Denim 027; 2 balls in Coral 086.

Colorful bandana bibs
SMC Baby Smiles Cotton; 100% Cotton, 92 m/100 yd, 25 g/0.8 oz.
1 ball each in Navy 50, Red 30, Sundance 22, White 01 and Apple Green 72.

Cute baby shorts
Debbie Bliss Baby Cashmerino; 55% Wool, 33% Acrylic, 12% Cashmere, 125 m/136 yd, 50 g/2 oz.
1 ball in Light Blue 202; 2 balls in Teal 203.

Complementary short sleeved sweater
Debbie Bliss Baby Cashmerino; 55% Wool, 33% Acrylic, 12% Cashmere, 125 m/136 yd, 50 g/2 oz.
2 balls in Denim 027; 1 ball in Coral 086.

Complementary long sleeved sweater
Debbie Bliss Baby Cashmerino; 55% Wool, 33% Acrylic, 12% Cashmere, 125 m/136 yd, 50 g/2 oz.
2 balls in Light Blue 202; 1 ball in Teal 203.

Sleepy sheep mobile
Debbie Bliss Fine Donegal; 95% Wool, 5% Cashmere, 380 m/415 yd, 100 g/3.5 oz.
1 ball each in Snowdrift 01, Brown 22 and Taupe 23.

Acknowledgements

Many thanks to the amazing team in London, especially Charlotte, for guiding me patiently and professionally through the process and putting my ideas and makes together in a book so beautifully. I am very thankful to my friends and family for supporting me in this international book adventure. Coby, Marja, Maartje, Tineke; thank you for your time, thoughts, moral support, and even crocheting with me Coby. And of course Jeroen and Annabel, without you this book would not have come to life. Thank you for your endless support, patience, ideas, and for putting up with a house full of yarn.

Love, Maaike

Thanks to the photographer, Simon Pask, and our models Eve Hawkins, Gemma Hickingbotham, Kayden Rajoo, Maisen Hall and Martha Minter, for bringing the projects to life.

Thank you to the following for supplying the wall coverings: Lohko Wallpaper (as seen on pages 21, 27, 42, 44, 47 and 53) from Scion, Stockist no: 0845 123 6805 www.scion.uk.com and Clouds Wallpaper (as seen on pages 15, 19, 32, 49, 84 and 95) from Albany at Wallpaperdirect.com.

Many thanks to Debbie Bliss and The Designer Yarns Group for so generously supplying the yarn for the projects.

Thanks also to Carol Meldrum, Lindsay Kaubi, Michelle Pickering and Christopher Summerville for their editorial work and index.